D0193507

Field of Compassion

Judy Cannato writes like a poet, visions like a mystic, and weaves a story that is original, provocative and inspiring. Her ability to integrate the wisdom of field theory, Christian compassion and personal narrative provides the reader with nourishment for intellect and spirit alike. A message of reassurance and hope for troubled times.

Diarmuid O'Murchu
Author of *Ancestral Grace*

I am absolutely enthralled with this book. I want to keep sitting inside its heart, to absorb more and more of the profound realities that Judy Cannato sets forth with such clarity and beauty.

Joyce Rupp
Author of *Open the Door*

Synthesizing the brilliant insights of our era's most significant scientists and spiritual teachers, Judy Cannato provides as well an effective process for embodying this new understanding. *Field of Compassion* is a gateway into the future of the human species.

Brian Swimme
Coauthor of *The Universe Story*

We are all called to the compassion in which we are already held, challenged to become what we already are. *Field of Compassion* engages us in this process. It is written with prophetic honesty, clarity and directness, urging us toward the global as well as personal transformation so desperately needed in our day. The book is gentle and yet strong, visionary and yet practical, pointing us ever toward the resources present, available, and simply awaiting our engagement. Yes, we can be agents of healing and compassion! *Field of Compassion* shows us how.

Barbara Fiand, S.N.D.
Author of *Awe-Filled Wonder*

Field of Compassion

How the New Cosmology
Is Transforming Spiritual Life

JUDY CANNATO

SORIN BOOKS / Notre Dame, Indiana

Scripture quotations are from the *New Revised Standard Version* of the Bible, copyright © 1993 and 1989 by the Division of Christian Education of the National Council of Churches of Christ in the U.S.A. Used by permission. All rights reserved.

© 2010 by Judy Cannato

All rights reserved. No part of this book may be used or reproduced in any manner whatsoever, except in the case of reprints in the context of reviews, without written permission from Sorin Books®, P.O. Box 428, Notre Dame, IN 46556-0428.

www.sorinbooks.com

ISBN-10 1-933495-21-9 ISBN-13 978-1-933495-21-7

Cover image © EROS/USGS/NASA/Phil Degginer/Alamy

Cover and text design by John R. Carson.

Printed and bound in the United States of America.

Library of Congress Cataloging-in-Publication Data
    Cannato, Judy.
      Field of compassion : how the new cosmology is transforming spiritual life / Judy Cannato.
      p. cm.
    Includes bibliographical references.
    ISBN-13: 978-1-933495-21-7 (pbk.)
    ISBN-10: 1-933495-21-9 (pbk.)
    1. Cosmology. 2. Consciousness. 3. Kingdom of God--Miscellanea. 4. Spiritual life. I. Title.
    BD701.C28 2010
    231.7--dc22
                            2009043967

■

With a grateful heart
for Bridget Pritchard, Carol Creek, and Carol Williams

■

Contents

Preface

This book is for mature readers only. It is not a self-help program. It is not about building self-esteem. It is not intended to convince you that God loves you. Neither is it an attempt to tell you about the many potentially deadly crises that beset our world. There are many books that deal with these topics, but we will take no time to deal with them here.

I want to be clear about where these pages are headed. The purpose of this book is twofold. First, I want to invite you, my fellow human being, to take up the challenge that is ours in this particular moment in human history, the invitation to transformation that will change the way our species lives. Second, I would like to suggest ways that we may walk through this new terrain together. We have no maps, nothing but the inner directions that seem to emerge as we engage the questions and risk moving toward the dream. Together we will learn where and how to go.

We must engage the new vision that is emerging within and among us with urgency. We haven't much time to turn things around. And turnaround will come not from an extraordinary rescue by an extraordinary deity. As we may have heard before, we are the ones we are waiting for. This is not to say that the Holy One is not present. On the contrary, it is because the Holy One is present that we are invited and challenged to respond. Karl Rahner said that we are "pressured" from within to evolve. That pressure is what we have always called the Holy Spirit. And the Spirit is creatively at work in this moment, urging us to evolve, to become a new kind of human being such as the world has rarely seen before. But what has been rare must now become commonplace.

Jesus invited his disciples to do the work that he empowered them to do, and more (Jn 14:12). What did he empower them to do? To love. To be communion for one another. To empower one another. To become free. To live with great passion and compassion. Jesus' empowerment of the disciples was not a supernatural distribution of gifts handed out in an exclusive way. Their empowerment came as they learned how to attend to the divine pressure from within, the Spirit, which allowed them to emerge as women and men who came to be more than they ever dreamed they could be. And what is "the more" that Jesus suggested the disciples would do? Perhaps nothing more than this—to live so empowered with love that compassion and all its accoutrements become simply the way we all live. Learning to live from within that kind of empowerment is what this book is about.

In one sense, the "kingdom of God," to use Jesus' term, was not meant to be something extraordinary, and it certainly was not intended to be exclusive. It was intended to be ordinary, the norm, the usual way relationships and community are done. Each of us living out of our best self—perhaps unusual, but certainly not anything out of the realm of possibility—was Jesus' dream. His vision, compelled by the Spirit within him, was what motivated his every word and action. He gave his life, not only his dying, but his living, to that vision. And in this moment of time it becomes clear that all that he lived for and hoped for and died for—the whole of the gospel—is what will guide us through the days ahead.

I also want to be clear that while I write from a Catholic Christian perspective, I do so in a way that includes all of us. Our great religious traditions have at their heart the conviction that we must live in peace and love, and that we cannot do so without the aid of the transcendent and sacred dimension of reality. So while I write from within my own tradition, I do so with the awareness that the pressure of the Spirit from within is a universal phenomenon, and no matter what images or languages we use to communicate our experience of the Spirit, each and every one of us is invited to be, each of us already *is*, an essential component of one Earth community—a Field of Compassion that embraces all.

Acknowledgments

There are very rich and powerful morphogenic fields in my life, and I wish to acknowledge particular ones here because they have been such a support not only in the writing but in challenging days in my life. My family has been there at every turn, and I want to thank each one: my husband Phil, Phil and Nicole, Doug, PJ, Kylie, and Gabrielle, my mother Lucille Lemaster and sister Linda Fraley, Frank and Betsy Cannato, Dr. Carrie Lee, Jenn Harte, and Melissa Ujcic. Your help and support that have come in so many ways have seen me through. Thank you.

One of the greatest blessings in my life is to be an associate member of the Congregation of St. Joseph. The charism and spirituality of this community sustains my heart. To the Sisters of the Congregation of St. Joseph, especially the members living in the founding community in Cleveland, I say thank you once again for all your love and support and for being "home." My thanks also goes to the St. Joseph communities in London, Ontario, and Llantarnam Abbey in Cwmbran, Wales. Your continued welcome is a delight. And I want to recognize the members of my Renewed Local Community and Chrysalis Mission Circle. My gratitude to and for you runs deep.

There are those who have offered support in so many and varied ways: Carol Creek; Carol Williams; Rita Petruziello, C.S.J.; Kathleen Kilbane, C.S.J.; JoAnne Skullin; Elizabeth Almeida; Pat Kozak, C.S.J.; Mary Southard, C.S.J.; Katheen McCluskey, C.S.J.; Nate Sears; Marianne Race, C.S.J.;

Mary Ellen Gondeck, C.S.J.; Dr. Joan Nuth; Liz Woconish; Dr. Keith Jordan; Paddy O'Flynn; Pat Creek; and Bridget Pritchard. Thank you for all the ways you have been present. And finally, my thanks to Bob Hamma and Patrick McGowan from Sorin Books/Ave Maria Press for nurturing the book along the way.

Introduction

Once in a while a story comes along that captures everything—what our lives are about, what we strive for, why we do what we do, where we hope we are headed. I recently heard such a story, one that in its simple detail has touched my heart and become rooted in my psyche. As I continue to integrate its images, the story settles my energy and holds my intention. In its simplicity it encapsulates other narratives that define me, and in its power expresses what I believe humankind is to be about at this time in our history—transformation. Here is the story:

One of the responsibilities of Nate Sears, a landscaper working at a housing complex on Cape Cod, is to check the piers at the adjacent beach for storm damage. One morning he was doing just that when he spotted a ten-foot pilot whale coming toward shore. He watched for a moment. He then saw a second whale, then a third, each one heading for land. Stunned at first, Nate watched the approach of the whales with awe. Then his concern took over. Since it is not unusual for whales to beach themselves on Cape Cod, Nate knew that this was the probable intent of these large, gentle mammals. He summoned a neighbor, who ran to call the National Sea Shore Service. Knowing that the whales were coming so fast that they would be on the beach before help could arrive, Nate quickly threw off his shoes and socks, rolled up his pant legs, and waded out in the direction of the first whale. He caught up with it in waist-deep water on a sand bar. The whale was thrashing about, and he could see cuts on its body from its batter with the sand. Moved solely by instinct, Nate placed his hands on the whale and held them there. The thrashing stopped. The whale became completely still. Nate said in that moment he became aware that this was the whale's first encounter with the human species. It seems that both human and whale were operating on instinct, each trusting the other in an encounter that neither had experienced before.

After the whale had grown calm, Nate gently turned it around and pointed it away from shore. The whale began to swim back out to sea. Losing no time, Nate approached the second whale. Again, he simply placed his hands on the creature and its thrashing stopped. Once this second whale grew still, Nate turned it away from shore. It, too, began to swim out. By this time members of the National Sea Shore Service arrived, and they helped Nate turn the third whale back.

Frequently, whales that threaten to beach themselves and are rescued come ashore in another location. That does not seem to be the case here. For whatever reason, the whales returned to their natural habitat without further incident. Although there is no proof, I think it was their encounter with Nate's energy and his willingness to simply hold them in their travail that made the difference.

Nate's actions—simply holding each whale until it was still, then gently turning the creatures until they were reoriented and able to navigate on their own once again—saved three whales that day. But to me, his actions are far more significant than he likely imagines. What he did on the beach is instructive for all of us, providing an image that is significant for the intentional process of transformation to which we are called.

The Call to Transformation

We find ourselves in a world with whale-sized issues, huge matters that seem unrestrained, threatening to not only go out of control, but take us down as well. Poverty, war, environmental crises, political conflict, and social divisions, as well as crises of trust in the very systems that were created to safeguard and protect humankind, are all huge issues that have a life and energy of their own. Disasters such as the great tsunami, earthquakes in Iran and Pakistan, hurricanes in the United States, and mudslides in Guatemala tug at our emotions and our resources. And at a time when we have both the supplies and capacity to distribute aid with unprecedented speed to the most remote locations, humane response is often hindered by inhumane policies or politics.

Our roles in the ongoing crises vary. Much of the time we seem to be part of gigantic systems that, while intended to address human or environmental needs, have shadowy underbellies that negate some aspects of the good they do. Government agencies and religious and social institutions often inadvertently create problems as well as solve them. At times these systems seem like whales with their sonar gone awry, thrashing wildly out of control. Sometimes we are pulled along for the ride; at other times we recognize that we are the whales by virtue of our connection to and participation in them, however reluctant that may be.

While it is necessary to be aware of how our institutions are and are not working and to critique them carefully and regularly, it is not productive to heap blame on or to disdain the agencies and institutions that have been formed out of our own best values. The simple fact is that everything has its shadow side. No person or institution escapes that reality. On the other hand, we are, like it or not, responsible for our shadows' consequences. As we mature both individually and as a species, we are summoned to recognize our shadows and remedy the problems they incur as best we can. This process is fundamental to transformation.

Besides recognizing that there are institutions or other collective forces that have strayed off course, losing their bearings, it is also necessary to recognize that we live in a time of unprecedented resourcefulness and creativity. That we have technological and material resources is abundantly clear. But we also have the resources of expanded consciousness and creativity that can be summoned to meet the needs of the day. We have at our disposal conscious awareness of the connectedness of all life and the opportunity for creative responses to the whales that threaten to beach themselves and thus threaten the life of us all.

While recognizing that simply by being alive and conscious we are part of the movement of whales threatening to throw themselves ashore, we must also acknowledge that we are the rescuers, the ones available and equipped to respond to the crises at hand. We can and must "save the whales"— and in doing so we also save ourselves.

Set in this context, Nate's story is instructive. Finding himself in an unfamiliar and unique situation, Nate responded in the moment, acting out of his own experience, following his instincts, intuitively doing the next right thing. Recognizing that time was of the essence, he trusted his ability to respond to the unknown in a way that was not only life-saving, but life-giving, both for himself and the whale. The incident may seem small, and some may even consider it insignificant, but what Nate did, what he participated in that day, held the essence of transformation—wading out to the cusp of the known/unknown, responding in care and kindness to the challenge of the moment, holding the tangible manifestation of the challenge in his hands, imparting his energy, and redirecting the movement.

What if we place ourselves in Nate's story, which in truth is our story, too? Suppose we imagine ourselves on the shore, walking on the pier, spotting the first whale, then the second, and then the third. Once we recognize what is happening, we call for help, run to the beach, take off our shoes and socks, and make our way out to the whale. Our hands encounter the sleek wetness of the huge mammal's body. Avoiding the thrashing of the tail, bloody from battering the sand, we hold our hands in place and, through our own wet palms, feel the whale's body begin to relax. Once it has grown completely still, we use all the strength we can muster to turn the whale's body around, pointing its head toward sea. Firmly we push and feel it budge off the sand, float free, then, with its bearings intact, head back to its home.

What would we feel in that moment, standing there in waist-deep water, exhausted from the physical struggle, perhaps even trembling at the emotional intensity of the experience? How would this encounter change us? How would it change the world? What if there were many whales—and many others to help us in the necessary task at hand? What if we were successful in our efforts—and as a result the entire Earth community transformed?

The Challenge of Transformation

Change that leads to transformation is rarely ever top-down, but more often inside-out. Great movements have begun with single conscious acts that somehow sound a vibration that resonates in the whole. We believe that such things can happen—that a single person can make an exceptional difference. But I think we also tend to believe that those who do so have been hand-selected by a God who is much too choosy to choose us. We tend to believe that most of us cannot and do not make much of a difference in the great scheme of things. The reality is that, noticed or not, every conscious act that gives witness to new possibilities and greater awareness contributes to the transformation of the whole. There is no insignificant thought, word, or action. Each act of courage and strength shifts the energy and increases the potential for others to become aware, too. No matter what we do, we are always affecting the energy around us, in either a negative or positive way. Why should we not then become aware of our power and choose consciously rather than unconsciously how we will shape our world?

Making consistent choices out of ever-growing awareness creates a spirit, a field of energy that catches others up and invites them in. We know this intuitively. Creating a field of kindness or care with intentionality produces an environment fecund with healing, allowing us to move out of our egocentric and fear-based behavior and into the kind of refulgent living that is at the heart of what Jesus means when he says, "I came that you might have life, and have it to the full." Life to the full is possible—but not without our choosing it one small action at a time.

Morphogenic Fields

The work of British biologist Rupert Sheldrake is fascinating, particularly his concept of morphogenic fields. According to his hypothesis, genetic material alone cannot account for the development of living systems. Sheldrake proposes that systems are surrounded by non-visible fields that carry information or memory from one generation to the next, thus making a new behavior pattern easier to learn.

The hypothesis of morphic resonance (the influence of like upon like) suggests that the human person and the systems to which humans belong are much more than what can be measured by standard empirical procedures. We are not merely personalities contained in a defined body, like water carried in a bucket. Rather, the human person is a field of energy and information rooted in the body but extending out from the body, interacting with the energy and information of others. None of us is a discreet, separate unit, but an integrated system of interactions and relationships connected to all.

What makes human beings unique is that we are self-aware. We have the capacity to notice and attend to the kind of energy and information we receive and transmit. Equally significant is that we can alter our energy and information fields by the choices we make. *Field of Compassion* rests on the conviction that we can become increasingly aware of who we are and how we influence our environment, and that we can and must make choices that are life-giving for all.

Using the image of the morphogenic field as a template, we can look at the mission of Jesus. Although he never could have used these words, Jesus was about creating a morphogenic field, one in which love is the standard operating procedure and genuine concern for the other is the behavioral norm. Thought, words, and activity are to be molded by this loving concern, a way of living that comes from conversion from egocentricity to love.

Jesus was unrelenting in his pursuit of what he called the "kingdom of God," a phrase that may also be translated as the "realm of God." Jesus never ceased inviting anyone who would listen—as well as those who would not—into this realm that was clearly not intended to be here-after but here-now. The realm of God was first of all to be characterized by a way of living in which all were included, a dangerously revolutionary idea in a religious culture that had hundreds of rules and regulations that only the elite could hope to keep. No one was left out or left behind, unless they chose to be. This was perhaps the most scandalous of Jesus' teachings, because it was a face-to-face confrontation with the spirituality of exclusion that ruled the day.

The realm of God that Jesus preached and died for was one that was known for its kindness and generosity, its compassion and healing. There was no one deemed outside the love of the Holy One whom Jesus called "Father." No one was excluded from fellowship, not the rich or poor, male or female, slave or free. Jesus went beyond superficial divisions and called for a culture of compassion.

Compassion changes everything. Compassion heals. Compassion mends the broken and restores what has been lost. Compassion draws together those who have been estranged or never even dreamed they were connected. Compassion pulls us out of ourselves and into the heart of another, placing us on holy ground where we instinctively take off our shoes and walk in reverence. Compassion springs out of vulnerability and triumphs in unity.

Field of Compassion is about the convergence of two streams: first, the promise of the realm of God as Jesus seems to have envisioned it; and second, the concept of morphogenic fields. As these streams converge, they create something new. What if we experiment with the notion that what Jesus was about was the creation of just such a morphogenic field, one that resonates with love and draws others like a magnet? What if we could intentionally contribute to the fashioning of a field in which attitudes and speech and action flow out of the very best that human beings can be? What if we with great intentionality take up the challenge to love God and neighbor with all our heart, mind, soul, and strength? What kind of morphic resonance would that create? How would we change? How would the world change?

I am not implying that Christian living up to this point has been a failure. The very place of possibility where we stand today is the result of morphic resonance created long ago and passed on to us in ever-new ways. What I am suggesting is that because of the critical condition of planetary life today, we need to recognize that the only possibility for the salvation of the whole planet will come from a ground-swell of compassion that changes destructive systems into life-giving communities in which we all live life to the full. Rather than contradict our religious tradition, such a movement would be a sign of its fulfillment.

We return to Nate's story: each one of us stands on a shore, on the cusp of the known and unknown. Each one of us encounters systems that have strayed off course. Each of us has the capacity and power to risk an encounter that brings peace and calm, healing and love. As we commit and remain faithful to the task at hand, we will begin to notice that we are not alone on the shore. To our left and to our right, all along the shore line, others are there, equally committed to risk and rescue, and faithful amidst the present crisis. Not only do we resonate with care and compassion, others do as well, and together we become a force to be reckoned with, one that not only changes the direction of the whales, but one that affects transformation that gives life to the whole of creation.

The plan of *Field of Compassion* is to assemble a variety of pieces, ones that hopefully will form a coherent whole. Chapter 1 addresses the significance of story and the ways in which stories shape our lives, both individually and collectively. The Universe Story is one that invites us to see the world differently and challenges us to change. Chapter 2 introduces the topic of morphogenic fields, an image that helps us hold the Universe Story a little more tangibly. This chapter also discusses morphic resonance and the four characteristics of holons. Chapters 3 and 4 begin to show the resonance between the Universe Story and the Christian story, particularly through the work of theologian Karl Rahner.

The morphogenic field that Jesus called the "kingdom of God" is the focus of chapter 5, a term that Neil Douglas-Klotz says can be translated as the "kindom of Unity." Chapters 6, 7, and 8 introduce three emerging fields that influence the development of a Field of Compassion. Chapter 6 examines the work of Susanne Cook-Greuter, who describes postautonomous ego development, or Unitive consciousness, that is emerging in larger numbers across the globe. Chapter 7 discusses what happens to the brain during meditation and how that contributes to growth in consciousness and ego development. The practice of meditation is a helpful tool in transformation because it teaches us to move to the place of witness, which assists us in becoming free from egocentricity. Chapter 8 discusses the power of intention. Lynne McTaggart's work on intentionality suggests that our thoughts and energy are always affecting reality, and the implication is that we need to set intentions mindfully and with care.

Chapter 9 begins to weave together the various strands— the significance of stories and the engagement of the emerging powers that are ours. Chapter 10 suggests some of the characteristics that are fundamental to the new consciousness, while chapter 11 speaks to the centrality of love and examines four stances that are essential for maintaining a Field of Compassion. Chapter 12 offers some final thoughts about the nature of the challenge to live in a new way.

Each chapter concludes with "A Contemplative Pause" that invites reflection on the topic that has been discussed. The purpose of the pause is to help integrate insights and apply them to one's personal life. Some may want to journal these reflections, while others may simply sit with the questions for a while without any kind of formal response. The point is to allow the information of the chapter to become part of the whole of you, to allow it to become more than a mind exercise.

Each Contemplative Pause begins with an examination of three Rs that may be of benefit as you move into reflection. The three Rs are intended to guide you to a contemplative witnessing of your own inner space, to assist noticing what is going on within you.

The first R is "resonance." What part of what you have read rings true with your own experience and affirms what you know to be true?

The second R is "resistance." Is there incongruity between what you have read and what you hold as true? Is there something that you don't want to see or hear, something that grates against your normal way of viewing things? Is there something that makes you want to dig in your heels or turn away?

The third R is "realignment." As a result of what you have read, has something shifted in you? Has something reconfigured so that you may live out of a slightly different place? What has shifted, what is different?

It is important to approach these three Rs without judgment. Judgment, whether "positive" or "negative"—especially what we deem "negative"—engages the ego, the part of our personality that is rooted in fear, the place in us that is insecure and wants to make itself safe by controlling what comes into our experience. Therefore, to avoid allowing the ego to take over the reflection, make no judgments about your response. Simply witness what is occurring: "Hmm . . . I notice that I am judging." "Hmm . . . I notice that I am angry." "Hmm . . . there I go again, being afraid"— or whatever emotion or experience is arising. Witness contemplatively, without assessment, and move on. This kind of noticing is at the heart of the practice of meditation, where we learn to simply witness what is arising without judgment or any other kind of engagement.

Following the suggestions for reflection, there will be a prayer that is a possible response to what you have integrated. Each of us prays in a different way, and the written prayer is simply one form that may be helpful. If you find it more useful to pray in a different way, to dance or sing or write a poem, please do! What is significant is that we are joining our energies and participating in our own creative ways in order to create and maintain a Field of Compassion.

chapter one

The Significance of Story

We are situated in a web of life. The same currents that run through our human blood also run through the swirling galaxies and the myriad of life-forms that pervade this planet: one and the same evolutionary current moves through all—a single self-transcending current of all-pervading energy that brings new life out of seeming catastrophe.

Ilia Delio

This we know. The earth does not belong to people. People belong to the earth. This we know. All things are connected. Whatever befalls the earth, befalls the people of the earth. We did not weave the web of life. We are but a mere strand in it. Whatever we do to the web, we do to ourselves.

Chief Seattle

Speak the story, whisper to the Earth,
touch the moments, blessings of rebirth.
Taste the wonders, the fragrances, the fears,
See Love's unfolding echo through the years.

Miriam Martin, P.B.V.M.

We understand our lives in and through stories. Some of the stories we live are archetypal, that is, universal in scope, and we share them with many others. These are the stories that guide our cultures and social groupings. Frequently unspoken, they are the bones on which we hang the flesh of our lives. They focus our awareness, are foundational to our purpose, and help shape our meaning. They guide our moral choices and suggest how we enter into relationships.

In addition to archetypal stories, we each have highly personal narratives that we have fashioned to tell who we are and how we have come to be who we are. The parents and siblings who inhabited our early years, our successes and failures, the births and deaths, the traumas and dreams, the loves and betrayals—all of them weave together to form the personal story that both consciously and unconsciously influences every move we make. It is possible to view our lives as a composite of stories—of the archetypal, universal stories that we experience collectively, and the individual and unique stories that have come with our personal lives.

Spoken or unspoken, stories are powerful containers for the energy of our lives. We live out of our stories each and every day, and as we respond over and over again to their influence, we find that rituals emerge, some quite formally, as when we enter into liturgical celebration with a community. Most often they are not formal at all, but simply the habits of thinking and acting we develop as we live our personal stories one day at a time.

Besides giving form to ritual action, stories provide us with images—images that have the power to draw us more deeply into the story. Some images are more formal and carry energy for a community, like the symbol of the cross, or the yin-yang, or a physical place that has collective memory attached to it. These formal symbols hold archetypal meaning for a community and hold our deepest human experiences even as they help form them. Other images are more personal, particular to our own experience. They may be physical objects, or places, or inner visions that help organize our energy and commitment in a way that may or may not be related to a larger community. Still, they are potent as they engage our being and help fashion who we are and how we live.

Images have an interesting way of engaging our minds. What if I say, "Don't think of a purple teddy bear"? What happens? It seems that automatically our minds go to the image of a purple teddy bear, contrary to the words that were spoken. Something about a visual form carried in our imagination has power to move our minds and draw us in. According to Bill Harris, founder of Centerpointe Research Institute, "Your brain takes whatever you focus on as an invitation to make it happen."[1] This is a powerful assertion. The images that flow from the narratives that engage us will help form the reality that manifests in our lives. If this is true, and I believe that it is, the images that engage our imagination shape who we become. It happens all the time. We simply do not notice.

But what if we were to notice? What if we were to be intentional about engaging our energy in a story that we know has the power to change our lives? I am not saying that we do not have good and powerful stories that engage us already. But we now live in a global community, and it seems wise that a universal story, one that lets go of the ethnocentricity and egocentricity that run through our past stories, will allow us to live in a global community with a greater sense of connectedness to all.

Thomas Berry has said that our generation is one that is in-between stories. We are caught between the story that religion tells and the story that science tells. For many of us the stories have seemed to clash, and we have felt the need to choose one or the other, even as we intuitively may have sensed that there has to be a single story that embraces the whole of life. During the last several decades, a new story has indeed emerged, a new cosmology that brings matters of science and matters of faith into a space where they no longer need collide, but can complement each other and render a fuller picture of what is true. Ironically, in modern times it is science that has told us the story of how all life is connected in a fundamental way—a story that the world's mystics have been telling for centuries.

The story that has guided the lives of those of us with Christian roots is the gospel. It is a story of the Holy One's ongoing love affair with humanity. It is a story that recognizes that the divine breaks into human experience in tangible ways and invites us to become united with Love itself so that we may become lovers. It is a story that resonates well with other religious traditions, for a thread that weaves through them all is an awareness of the transcendent dimension of human experience and the need to offer a response that is grounded in compassion.

Francis of Assisi is reported to have said, "Preach the gospel at all times. When necessary, use words." Perhaps he knew that words can get in the way. Perhaps he knew that it is an image filled with energy that most effectively guides us and allows us to engage the story in a way that gives it flesh.

If the mind does indeed take us to that which we envision, then the vision we hold is the most essential component in living a fully awakened, fully engaged life. If compassion is the reality to which all of our experiences of the transcendent call us, then a story that lures us into compassion and an image that engages the whole of humanity into living as one diverse but interconnected community will allow us to evolve and manifest an awakened consciousness.

The Universe Story

The overarching narrative that has emerged as a result of modern scientific discoveries is called the Universe Story. It is a story of the origin and development of the universe that began with the Big Bang—what Brian Swimme calls the Flaring Forth—and continues in this very moment. It was in 2003 that Dr. Wendy Freedman and a team of astrophysicists, using information gathered by the Cosmic Background Explorer (COBE), was able to determine that the originating creative event occurred 13.7 billion years ago. All that exists in this universe lay in latent potential in that fecund moment.

Since the 1920s we have known that this universe of ours is expanding, spreading out uniformly in space. Recently, science has discovered that the expansion that is moving at an accelerating rate is propelled by something called Dark Energy, an invisible force that cannot be seen or measured in ordinary ways but is very real. We also know that a complementary force exists, Dark Matter, which helps hold the universe together. Dark Energy and Dark Matter comprise about 96 percent of the universe, with only 4 percent falling into the category we call "ordinary" matter.

The discoveries made in the field of astrophysics over the past few decades have been remarkable. Less than a century ago, it was thought that our own Milky Way galaxy was the only galaxy that existed. Distant galaxies that could be observed, like Andromeda, were described as nebula, just a smattering of cosmic material suspended in space. But in the 1920s Edwin Hubble, using his new hundred-inch telescope on Mt. Wilson in southern California, was able to see that Andromeda was a galaxy in its own right. Today we know that there are billions of galaxies, each with billions of stars, extending billions of light years out into space. In 1968, with the Apollo space mission, human beings for the first time experienced themselves as extraterrestrials, caught in awe and wonder by the sight of "the big blue marble" that is our home. Since the early 1990s instruments like the Hubble space telescope have brought to us brilliant images of cosmic matter that are so dazzling that they take our breath away. The sheer immensity and elegance of the universe we have come to experience is ineffable, its beauty beyond words.

The world of quantum physics contributes to the Universe Story as well. Prior to the discovery of quantum mechanics, Newtonian physics asserted that the atom, a word which means "indivisible," was the fundamental unit of matter. Scientists thought they had reached the bottom line of the material world and could therefore explain reality on that basis. But quantum physics turned that notion upside-down, demonstrating that atoms are not hard-boundaried units and that there is an entire world of sub-atomic particles that can be described as either particles or waves. And what scientists are now saying is that if we look down farther and farther, on smaller and smaller scales, what we come to is not some "thing," but something like information, thought, or consciousness.

Quantum physics also asserts that life emerges from what physicist David Bohm called the quantum vacuum. Bohm said, "There is one energy that is the basis of all reality."[2] According to Bohm, the quantum vacuum is the fundamental underlying reality of which everything in the universe is an expression—everything—including ourselves. Described as a vast sea in which all potentiality is present, from which every manifestation comes, the quantum vacuum has no particles, yet particles come about as its energy fluctuates. Brian Swimme has said that particles boil into existence out of sheer emptiness, and that is simply the way the universe works. Bohm also said that form is not the result of mechanical laws of physics and chemistry but emerges from the quantum vacuum.

It is no surprise then that a basic principle of quantum physics is that of nonlocality. Evidence demonstrates that objects can be affected in the absence of a local cause—in other words, we don't have to be "on location" to exercise influence on someone or something else. Physicist Danah Zohar says:

> At the subatomic level . . . correlation experiments have now been carried out many times on pairs of correlated photons, and the nonlocal influences that bind their "lifestyles" have been proved many times over. The photons' behavior patterns are so linked across any spatial separation—it could be a few centimeters, it could be all the way across the universe—that it appears as if there is no space between them.[3]

Emerging from the single quantum vacuum, it seems that we remain connected throughout our lives, bound together by a mysterious energy that makes all creation a single whole.

In 1969, Dr. Edward Lorenz, a mathematician and meteorologist from MIT, first described the Butterfly

Effect. Lorenz was working on calculations of weather patterns when he happened to switch to a calculator that carried out to a few more decimal points than the first one he was using. To his surprise, he obtained very different forecasts using the two calculators. His discovery tells us that the tiniest of perturbations—a movement as slight as the ruffle of a butterfly's wing—can change a system or energy pattern. Since each of us can be described as an energy pattern, the implications are profound.[4]

Another finding of quantum physics is the Observer Effect. The famous two-slit experiment, designed to find whether a photon is a particle or a wave, determined that when an experiment is set up to test for a particle, the photon manifests as a particle. When set up to test for a wave, the photon manifests as a wave. According to authors Ian Marshall and Danah Zohar:

> The quantum observer stands *inside* his or her observations, which themselves play an active role in bringing about the very reality they then look at. In a sense not yet fully understood, the quantum observer helps to *make* the world of his or her observations.[5]

We are always connected, no matter what the spatial distance, and our slightest movements affect others. Lynne McTaggart says it quite well:

> At our most elemental, we are not a chemical reaction, but an energetic charge. Human beings and all living beings are a coalescence of energy in a field of energy connected to every other thing in the world. The pulsating energy field is the central engine of our being and our consciousness, the alpha and the omega of our existence. There is no 'me' and 'not-me' duality to our

bodies in relation to the universe, but one underlying energy field.[6]

The Universe Story is a radically amazing one. It tells us that in some mysterious way we help bring about that which is manifested in the physical world. All life emerges from the same cosmic source, an initial creative event that continues to unfold moment by moment. Since we emerge from the same source, all creatures are part of a single community of life. Even as we live in such rich diversity, we are joined together at the most fundamental of levels.

In human beings there has emerged a unique consciousness that allows us to recognize our connectedness and to respond to the needs of the whole in a way that is life-giving for all. In this moment of history, we are coming to see the disastrous consequences of living in ignorance of the fact that we are joined to others in life. Some suggest that is too late for our species or that we simply do not have the will to operate out of a different paradigm. I believe it is not too late, that a newly emergent consciousness is already here. We simply need to learn how to activate the power we have in order to make the changes we need.

The Universe Story, besides telling us that we are part of a single creation event, is an evolutionary one. Here I am speaking of evolution in its broadest sense, a dynamic process at the heart of the created world, characterized by increased diversity with greater, more complex consciousness. Creation is a single holistic system, and within the whole each and every holon (whole) has the capacity for self-transcendence, the capacity to become more than it presently is. Theologian Karl Rahner has said that "active self-transcendence" is actually the Spirit of God working from within creation, compelling it to evolve.

Field of Compassion is about living in a new way that is grounded in the Universe Story, with attention to the implication that all life is connected. It is about acknowledging that we all flow from a single source, call it quantum vacuum or Holy Spirit, and that what each of us does affects all the other wholes of which we are a part and all of the parts that make us whole. Our exploration together is concerned with living with the awareness of our connectedness and making choices that are life-giving for all. It is about casting off the vestiges of an old mechanistic paradigm and embracing and living out of a unitive consciousness that will make compassion our normal operating procedure. It is intended to get us out of the in-between place, no longer stuck between stories, no longer tethered to narratives that are divisive and harmful. It is meant to help us together grow in freedom so that we may participate creatively in that which is emerging around us and among us.

A CONTEMPLATIVE PAUSE

Settle into a quiet inner space, take a few deep relaxing breaths, and then, when you are ready, enter into the following exercises.

- I consider insights within me that have arisen throughout this chapter. Where is there resonance? Where is there resistance? Where is there realignment?

- What are the stories that shape and fashion my life—the bones on which I hang the flesh of my life? What are the archetypal or universal stories that guide my vision and choices? What are the uniquely personal stories that also weave themselves into my life and influence who I am? I invite what is unconscious to become conscious, and do not resist, so that I may know myself more fully and more truthfully.

- What are the images that guide my journey, draw my attention, and fashion my awareness? Do I see images that are not helpful because they interfere with my desire to become whole? What image do I choose to hold in my awareness so that I may move toward it and manifest it tangibly in my daily life? I remember that my mind takes whatever I focus on as an invitation to make it happen.

A PRAYER

Holy One, you have given us the gift of story in our lives, ways of understanding who we are, ways of making sense of our world, of finding meaning and knowing how to respond to all that happens in our lives. Please show us where our stories fall short or are too narrow, where they exclude rather than include, where they divide rather than unite. Help us to see where a story we live out of may go amiss of what is real, where it allows us to escape becoming whole, where it lets us live comfortably in fear. Fill us with your story, the story of unity and compassion and love. Fill us with images that energize us and give us hope and lead us to the fundamental truth that you have tried to teach us all along: we are all one. Amen.

chapter
two

Morphogenic Fields

Evolution goes beyond what went before, but because it must embrace what went before, then its very nature is to transcend and include, and thus it has an inherent directionality, a secret impulse, toward increasing depth, intrinsic value, increasing consciousness.

Ken Wilber

Insofar, then, as the higher order always embraces the lower as contained within it, it is clear that for the real event of self-transcendence the lower prepares for and is a prelude to this self-transcendence in the unfolding of its own reality and order. In its history it moves slowly towards that boundary which is then surpassed in the actual self-transcendence.

Karl Rahner

The Universe Story offers us great hope as a species. It is a story that tells us that the universe is a single evolutionary process, dynamic and organic, and that all life is fundamentally connected. In this story no one or no thing is excluded from the whole. In fact, the connectedness is so essential that the movement of one part affects the whole. Physicist Paul Dirac once said, "Pick a flower on earth and you move the farthest star."[1] We are truly one, even though we may have learned something quite different.

Embracing the Universe Story and all its implications can be a bit overwhelming. Seeing the Hubble space telescope images or hearing that the universe has billions of galaxies, each with billions of stars, stretches us to the limits of our imaginations. We cannot fathom the immensity of our cosmos, and to catch just a glimpse of that immensity catapults us head over heels into mystery. The gift of the Universe Story is that it sweeps away anything smaller. Narratives that make us little fall by the wayside. A difficulty we experience, however, is that the Universe Story is simply too big for us to hold, and we need something a bit smaller to help us touch all that immensity in a way that allows us to respond in tangible ways.

For me the image of the morphogenic field has served just this purpose. Rooted in the work of British biologist Rupert Sheldrake, it is an image that in many ways is simple to grasp, yet it is profound in its implications. It allows for tangibility and helps hold a newly emergent consciousness that is essentially beyond words at this point. In retreats and workshops over the last few years, I have used the image of a morphogenic field to explore the emerging new consciousness. What I have discovered is that I am not alone in finding the image, together with the understanding of morphic resonance, a helpful one. We are able to describe that which is emerging concretely enough to make it real—and a possibility within reach. We have been able to see that a new morphogenic field characterized by compassion is emerging, or else we would not be able to give it such detailed description. It is in the implementation of the fundamental characteristics of the field that there is great work to be done. The new consciousness is already here.

It seems that morphogenic fields are more easily understood through stories, so that is where I will begin. The following is from Rupert Sheldrake's work: In Southampton, England, in the early 1920s, a common species of bird called the blue tit was observed tearing the cardboard caps off milk bottles that had been delivered on neighborhood door steps. The birds would sip cream off the top, and some reports say that the small birds could be seen following the milkman as he made his deliveries from door to door. The first recorded incident of the cream sipping came in 1921. Amateur birdwatchers began to trace the habit, which continued to spread hundreds of miles away—surprising because blue tits seldom fly farther than fifteen miles from their nests. By 1947, the habit was ubiquitous throughout Britain and had also spread to Sweden, Holland, and Denmark. However, beginning in 1939–40, milk delivery in German-occupied Holland was halted, leaving the birds without access to their milk supply. Delivery did not resume until 1948, about five years longer than the life span of the blue tit. Yet within months of milk being delivered to doorsteps again, the habit returned, and within a year or two it was once more universal in Holland.[2] What explains the spread (and the resumption) of this habit?

Here is another of Sheldrake's stories: In the 1980s, Dr. Arden Mahlberg, a psychologist from Madison, Wisconsin, developed a variation of the Morse Code that should have been no more difficult to learn than the original version developed in 1838. Still, test subjects learned the old version much more quickly and accurately than the new.[3]

A woman who leads retreats in the Holy Land told me this story: A few years ago a group of students participating in a sabbatical program connected to the Catholic Theological Union in Chicago spent three months studying in the Middle East. While in Israel they visited the region known as the High Places, exploring the ruins of Tel Arad, an ancient city in the Negev region. Tel Arad had been inhabited by the Israelites in the eighth and ninth centuries BCE, and on this site there was a temple with a small Holy of Holies and a brick and rubble altar, where rituals that included animal sacrifice had taken place. Apparently a little bored with the archeological lectures, some of the students, as a joke, decided to "sacrifice" the youngest person in the group. He willingly climbed upon the altar and stretched himself out as part of the charade. Astonishingly, within seconds buzzards began circling overhead, even though the altar had not been used for sacrifice in over 2,700 years.

Another story: At the age of two, Nicholas Taylor, son of Frank and Dina, could sit in front of a computer and assemble his own version of Thomas the Tank Engine. He could navigate through the web site to select cars with names like Oliver, Percy, Rusty, or Spencer and string them together to make his own train. Like most of us, Nick's parents struggle a bit with computer technology. Where did their son get this ability—a skill so many young children seem to pick up so easily?

Psychologists discovered long ago that learning—whether it is a habit like that of the blue tit, the capacity to memorize new data, or the ability of young children to work with computers—is not inherited. That is, there is no genetic difference between one participant and the next. Sheldrake says that what we learn is held not in our brains but in morphogenic fields.

Fields

To understand morphogenic fields more completely, we must begin with an understanding of the concept of the "field."[4] A field can be described as a non-material region of influence that structures the energy of a system. A helpful example is the field around a magnet. It is non-material—we cannot touch it or see it, it is not embodied, yet we know it to be a real force that moves energy. The field has a region of influence, meaning that there is a place where it affects energy and a place where it does not. And it has influence. It affects matter and energy, it helps hold matter and energy in some way, even though there is not material contact.

Sheldrake writes that according to modern physics, fields are more fundamental than matter. Fields cannot be explained in terms of matter. Rather, matter is explained in terms of energy within fields.[5] Somehow a field holds energy and allows it to take form as matter. Another way to say this is that matter is energy bound within fields. As with a magnet, the field is both within and around the form that takes shape. Sheldrake asserts that a field is not a "thing" so much as it is information or a habit or memory. Asking the questions "Where do we store information?" and "Where do we keep our memories?" he in jest says that we have cut open quite a few brains and not found them there! What Sheldrake suggests is that our brains are more like radio receivers—that we tune in to information in the same way a radio tunes in to a station. For Sheldrake, information, habits, and memories are all held in morphogenic fields.

Morphogenic Fields

A morphogenic field, then, is a non-material region of influence within and around a particular form. It can be thought of as a field of information. A morphogenic field organizes the structure and the activity of a form or system. It holds the energy, keeping it coherent. Each form, system, or holon has its own morphogenic field. Each person is a morphogenic field, as is each group we belong to. There are morphogenic fields of atoms, cells, molecules, rabbits, elephants, petunias, oak trees, communities, and so on. Each type and level of existence can be described as a morphogenic field.

Each morphogenic field has its own distinctive characteristics and habits. Each has a different feel to it, a unique presence. Each preserves its own information and memories. Depending on its level of complexity, each has its own customs and beliefs and values. Each has its means of communication, its own language, as well as its own way of doing relationships. The behaviors associated with a particular morphogenic field become routine, almost like law, "the way we do things around here."

We can say then that it is a morphogenic field that helped hold the energy around the blue tits' milk-sipping skills, a morphogenic field that enabled subjects to learn the old Morse code more quickly than the new, a morphogenic field that held the vultures' memory of the High Places, a morphogenic field that allowed a two-year-old to be proficient at the computer. Over time, morphogenic fields begin to have a cumulative memory and become increasingly habitual, making it easier for those entering the field to learn its associated habits.

Morphic Resonance

An important term in understanding the workings of the morphogenic field is that of morphic resonance, essentially the influence of like upon like. Sheldrake says, "Morphic resonance takes place on the basis of similarity."[6] The greater the similarity a morphogenic field has to previous morphogenic fields, the greater influence it has on subsequently emerging fields. And the greater number of previous morphogenic fields that resonate with and feed into the new, the greater the morphic resonance will be. For example, as more and more blue tits (each one a morphogenic field) acquired the behavior of tearing caps off milk bottles, the stronger the morphic resonance, the greater and more powerful the emergent morphogenic field and its habits, and the easier it became for other blue tits to learn the behavior. The same goes for the morphogenic field of computers. The more morphic units participating or resonating, the easier the behavior may be acquired by those who are newly entering the field.

Each morphogenic field has a collective memory that helps shape what follows. "The coming into being of form," Sheldrake writes, "does not take place in a vacuum. All processes of development start from systems that are already specifically organized."[7] Since all past members of a field—whether a single bird, a person, or an organized group—contribute to the energy of the field, the influence or resonance increases as the number of participants increases. The structure that a particular field takes, then, depends on what has happened before and the exchange of information between or among fields.

According to Sheldrake, there is a non-energetic exchange of information that takes place between morphogenic fields. It is nonlocal in nature, meaning that morphic resonance involves a sort of "action at a distance" both in space and time.[8] Contact with a morphogenic field does not depend on physical proximity, in other words; its energy can be experienced and its influence felt over any spatial separation.

It is important to remember that morphogenic fields are grounded in the physical world. Like gravitational, electromagnetic, or quantum matter fields, morphogenic fields are related to matter. Fields are what interact with and organize the physical world.[9] This is not to say that the relationship between fields and matter is dualistic, with fields and matter being polar opposites. Rather, since matter is energy bound in fields, there is a mutuality of exchange, each intricately related to the other.

Morphogenic Fields and Holons

A subject related to morphogenic fields is the theory of holons, a word coined by Arthur Koestler in the 1960s and developed further throughout the work of Ken Wilber.[10] In essence, the theory of holons states that everything in the universe is a whole-part. Nothing is a whole apart from everything else, and nothing is a part separate from other wholes. The universe is composed of whole-parts. A whole atom is part of a whole molecule. A whole molecule is part of a whole cell. A whole letter is part of a whole word. A whole person is part of a whole community.

A helpful image for understanding holons is that of nesting dolls—one inside the other, inside the other, inside the other. A cell is nested in the molecule, the molecule is nested in the atom. This holds true for every level of complexity and demonstrates how all life is connected, with each stage of development emerging out of the one before it.

Holons are arranged in order of complexity, with the less complex having a broader expanse or greater numbers, and the more complex having more depth but fewer numbers. As we know, cells emerge from molecules, so there are more molecules than cells. Cells have greater complexity than molecules and therefore are placed at a higher order than molecules. Molecules have the greater expanse, while cells have the greater depth. This order of complexity is called a holarchy. Not to be confused with hierarchy, in which different values are placed on various levels with the top level controlling all below, a holarchy simply designates order of complexity, with the higher orders being nested in and therefore dependent on the lower. Remove any level of holons in a holarchy and all the holons above will be destroyed. All holons are interdependent.

Characteristics of Holons

Each holon has four characteristics, which can be thought of in pairs: self-preservation and self-adaptation, and self-transcendence and self-dissolution. Self-preservation is the capacity for autopoiesis or autonomy. It is the impulse that works within the acorn as it becomes the oak tree or the movement within the infant who crawls and then walks. Each holon has its own particular wholeness and maintains its own form or structure from within. Miriam Therese MacGillis describes this capacity:

> Whether we speak of a giraffe or an atom of carbon, the activity of each is proper to its own order of complexity. Each carries within it an interior depth, a special quality, a mystery. Each of the individual creatures of the different species has its own interiority. Even beings that were previously considered to be inert carry within them an interior depth. Therefore, each has its

own identity and is not to be considered merely as one object among others.[11]

Self-preservation is an energy within each morphogenic field/ holon enabling it to sustain its identity, hold its boundaries, and act freely.

The second characteristic of the holon, one held in tension with self-preservation, is that of self-adaptation. Each holon is not simply a whole, but is part of a larger whole. Self-adaptation is the capacity to accommodate and adapt to other holons. Another word is communion. Thomas Berry says:

> For every reality of the universe is intimately present to every other reality of the universe and finds its fulfillment in mutual presence. The entire evolutionary process depends on communion. Without this fulfillment that each being finds in beings outside itself, nothing would ever happen in the entire world. There would be no elements, no molecules, no life, no consciousness.[12]

Twelfth-century Rhineland mystic Hildegard of Bingen spoke of this capacity when she said that God has arranged everything in the universe in consideration of everything else. We know from quantum theory that we live in a web of interconnections, each influencing and being influenced by everything else. Brian Swimme says it so well: "Nothing is itself without everything else." We are participants in one another's lives at every level of being.

Self-preservation and self-adaptation work together, ideally with a creative tension between them. Each holon must preserve itself, maintaining its integrity, its own particular wholeness, as a prerequisite for being in relationship with other wholes and other parts. A molecule must retain its identity as a molecule in order to adapt to or be in communion with both atoms (lower on the holarchy) and cells (higher on the holarchy). As humans we experience this tension all the time, balancing personal and communal needs. Whenever there is more of one, there is less of the other, and often that is appropriate. What is key is maintaining the capacity to choose freely where we concentrate the most energy at any given time.

A third capacity of holons is self-transcendence. Each and every holon has the capacity to become more than it presently is. For the human person, self-transcendence is a kind of orientation toward a horizon that forever recedes, even as we move toward it. Elizabeth Johnson writes:

> The orientation to the horizon is part of the life of every person whether they pay attention to it or not. It is not one particular experience among others, but the ultimate depths of every other distinctly personal experience, the very condition that makes them all possible. Because where would we be if there were only a limited number of questions we could ask, a set number of free decisions we could make, a restricted amount of beauty we could enjoy, or a quota on tears?[13]

Self-transcendence involves our capacity to grow and develop, to hold and to envision, to dream a dream and fulfill it in tangible ways. It underpins our ability to experience quantum leaps in insight and awareness.

Each holon has the capacity to evolve into something more complex, to respond to the tension between self-preservation and self-adaption with creativity, and to do so over and over and over again, asking the next question and moving steadily toward the ever-receding horizon. Each new step is nested in the old, like the child's ability to walk that transcends but does not destroy its ability to crawl. And whenever a holon transcends a former way of being in the world, it evolves to a new level of self-preservation and self-adaption as well.

There is another capacity of holons that is held in tension with self-transcendence, and that is self-dissolution. We all have bodies that fail. We experience dyings that encroach upon our living. We have egos that give way to fear and lock us in self-absorption. We often experience a pull toward the negative, a resistance to growth even when we desire it. This is what Paul described in his letter to the Romans: "I don't understand my own actions. For I do not do what I want, but I do the very thing I hate" (Rom 7:15). In each aspect of our lives—whether it is primarily physical, emotional, psychological, or spiritual—we experience a pull toward dissolution and negation that requires an ever-present vigilance.

If we are aware, the tension we notice as we respond to experiences of self-dissolution can sharpen our consciousness and facilitate growth in freedom. Paradoxically, it seems that within experiences of self-dissolution there are also opportunities for self-transcendence; a single incident can provide a growing awareness of both. And the gift of self-dissolution is that it gives us practice in the little dyings that are integral to transformation.

Morphogenic Fields and Story

The purpose of this exploration of morphogenic fields and holons is to propose a unified image that will facilitate integration of the Universe Story. Morphogenic fields are holons; holons are morphogenic fields. The image of the morphogenic field/holon and the process of morphic resonance complement the Universe Story. First, both stories are evolutionary. In each there is a dynamic, creative development that involves greater complexity and concomitantly greater consciousness. The present is nested in the past. Second, both are grounded in the material world yet provide a model for understanding the greater complexities that emerge out of the physical matter, including consciousness. Third, both the Universe Story and the concept of morphogenic fields provide images for the connectedness of creation that we know is our fundamental reality. We are a single organic whole, a knowing that when integrated asks us to live differently, perhaps to become a new species altogether.

In our own process of evolution, human beings have acquired self-reflective consciousness. We call ourselves *homo sapiens sapiens*, the ones who know that we know. What comes with our kind of knowing is freedom, the capacity to imagine options and choose from among them. In his letter to the Galatians, Paul writes that it is for freedom that Christ set us free (Gal 5:1). Not for love or service or community or justice or peace, but for freedom, in which all these other virtues and capacities are rooted.

Freedom is the floor upon which all of these virtues and capacities dance. Love, service, community, justice, or peace cannot be if they are not rooted in freedom, for anything less than freedom will distort them and drain them of their power. I think that it is possible to describe the kind of freedom at the heart of the gospel as "the capacity to choose to engage in the process of the evolution of consciousness." We have the capacity to make choices that will evolve us, both personally and as a species. We have the capacity to engage in the management of the whale-sized issues that confront us, most of our own making. We have the capacity to cooperate with the unfolding of the universe, a process driven by grace, which invites us to be co-creators. We have the capacity to choose to live out of a new story grounded in life-giving images that facilitate our own emergence.

This is where the image of the morphogenic field is so helpful. We participate and evolve into new morphogenic fields all the time. Each of us is a morphogenic field participating, influencing, and being influenced by other morphogenic fields. What if we were to be intentional about maintaining an emerging morphogenic field? What if we were to engage our energies as consciously as possible in order to influence and help manifest this new emerging consciousness, a consciousness rooted in the past, yet filled with promise for our species and all life on our planet? Would this not be resonant with the call to live in freedom so that we might experience the depth of love? In such a critical moment in our own history, can we do anything but this?

It is my conviction that we can and must participate consciously in strengthening the morphogenic field of new consciousness that has emerged. The new field is here; it is already filled with energy; and when we become aware and attend to it, it lures us in with its power. Our past experiences have prepared us for its coming, and our conscious participation strengthens its energy. It is a morphogenic field rooted in and characterized by love—what we may call a Field of Compassion.

A CONTEMPLATIVE PAUSE

Settle into a quiet inner space, take a few deep relaxing breaths, and then, when you are ready, enter into the following exercises.

- I consider insights within me that have come throughout this chapter. Where is there resonance? Where is there resistance? Where is there realignment?

- I consider myself as a morphogenic field. What are the characteristics that are unique to me? What are the habits and memories I hold, the customs, beliefs, values, languages, and ways of entering into relationships? How do I describe my energy?

- I consider the morphogenic fields within me—the morphogenic fields of sub-atomic particles, atoms, of molecules, cells, tissues—the entire physical holarchy present within me. What do I notice?

- I consider the collective morphogenic fields of which I am a part, from family and friends to larger communal structures, and social and cultural units such as ethnic group or nationality. How do I exchange energy or information with each, and how does each energize or inform me?

- How do I experience self-preservation, self-adaptation, self-transcendence, and self-dissolution in my life? Is the tension between self-preservation and self-adaptation creative or draining? What are my experiences of self-transcendence? What are my experiences of self-dissolution?

A PRAYER

Holy Heart of the Universe, help me to see myself in relation to all that is. Help me to recognize the ways that my energy touches all that is, the ways my habits and words affect all the wholes of which I am a part, and all the parts that make me whole. Empower me, that I may embrace the capacity for self-transcendence as I negotiate the tension between self-preservation and self-adaptation. Allow me to learn from experiences of self-dissolution, and enable me to grow in the capacity to live in freedom. May the morphogenic field that I am be life-giving to all. Amen.

The Universe Story and Christian Story

In a way without parallel in Christian history we have rediscovered a God who is totally immersed in our history, our suffering, our hope. . . . Above all else, we have entered a time when the fundamental character of humanity and the universe is being revealed as that of exchange and interdependence.

Robin Green

I have the immense joy of being [human], a member of a race in which God became incarnate. As if the sorrows and stupidities of the human condition could overwhelm me, now I realize what we all are. And if only everybody could realize this! But it cannot be explained. There is no way of telling people that they are all walking around shining like the sun.

Thomas Merton

Each evolving morphogenic field emerges from previous fields, influenced by the presence of morphic resonance.

Many people, when they begin to recognize the implications of the Universe Story, ask questions like these: Where is God in the new story? Where is Jesus? Does this contradict the Christian tradition? How do the two stories—the one faith tells and the one science tells—connect? These are significant questions that challenge us to re-think what we believe in light of what science knows. I recall a friend, a very bright man with a deep interior life, who years ago left the institutional church. "I just can't keep checking my brain at the door," he said. Despite his experience, one that many share, the Second Vatican Council recognized the impact of the Universe Story: "And so [humankind] substitutes a dynamic and more evolutionary concept of nature for a static one, and the result is an immense series of new problems calling for a new endeavor of analysis and synthesis" (*Gaudium et Spes* 5).

The good news is that there is plenty in the Christian tradition—the Christian morphogenic field—that resonates with the Universe Story. Insights from our theology and mystical tradition converge with the Universe Story and become key elements of the new emerging consciousness. This makes Christian faith deeply relevant to the new morphogenic field that has developed. The purpose of this chapter is to describe the Christian morphogenic field in a way that demonstrates its resonance with the Universe Story. It is not intended to be exhaustive, but rather set the context for talking about the newly emerging morphogenic Field of Compassion.

The First Church "Council"

First, it is necessary to look at how theology is done. A meeting of many of the earliest Christian leaders described in Acts 15 is often called "the First Church Council." Councils, according to the Church, are theologically definitive. Even though Jesus was primarily concerned with calling people to a way of relating to others and the Holy—a new consciousness—he could not possibly have anticipated all the issues that would arise as the infant movement began to grow. A dynamic that began with the early church was the grappling with issues that arose when followers of Jesus and their leaders negotiated the transition from Judaism to what would later be called Christianity.

The story of the First Church "Council" begins by saying that there were some men from Judea preaching, "Unless you are circumcised according to the custom of Moses, you cannot be saved." In other words, there were some followers who were teaching that Gentile believers must first become Jews. When Paul and Barnabas heard of this, they "had no small discussion and debate with them." Following the local dialogue, Paul, Barnabas, and some of the other disciples were appointed to go to Jerusalem, to meet with the apostles and elders there about the matter.

The church at Jerusalem welcomed Paul and Barnabas and were glad to hear what God had being doing in their midst. The discussion began again, with some believers of the Pharisee party claiming, "It is necessary to circumcise Gentile believers and to charge them to keep the law of Moses." The apostles and elders continued to talk. "After there had been much debate," Peter stood up and spoke about how he had witnessed God granting the Holy Spirit to the Gentiles "just as [God] did to us." Peter told the others that God "made no distinction between us and them, but cleansed their hearts by faith." He then questioned why they would make trial of God "by putting a yoke upon the neck of the disciples which neither we nor our fathers have been able to bear?" He then added, "But we believe that we shall be saved through the grace of the Lord Jesus, just as they will." After hearing Peter, the assembly kept silence. Then they listened to Barnabas and Paul tell of their ministry among the Gentiles.

After Barnabas and Paul had finished speaking, James replied, saying, "Brethren, listen to me. Simeon has related how God first visited the Gentiles, to take out of them a people for his name, and with this the words of the prophets agree. It is written, 'After this I will return, and I will rebuild the dwelling of David, which has fallen; I will rebuild its ruins, and I will set it up, that the rest of men may seek the Lord, and all the Gentiles who are called by my name, says the Lord, who has made these things known from of old.'" After having spoken, James then renders his judgment: "We should not trouble the Gentiles who turn to God, but should write to them to abstain from the pollutions of idols and from unchastity and from what is strangled and from blood."

This passage from Acts illustrates how Christian theology is done. First, it is rooted in human life, the daily experience of those whose intention it is to respond to the holy within the context of a human relationship with the risen Christ. Implicit in this conversation is the disciples' appeal to the words of Jesus, both before and after the resurrection, as well as their lived experience of Jesus as they became his followers. They report how they have witnessed the Holy Spirit working, seemingly unbound by expectation or customs. In their discernment they appeal to both tradition and to scripture, in this case to the wisdom of the prophets. They did not appear to restrict their discussion but allowed everyone involved in the matter to speak. They kept silence. Then, and only then, after asking the difficult questions and entering into silence and discussion and debate, there came an interpretation—as broad as possible so as to facilitate an experience of the risen Christ rather than restrict it. This is the pattern of theological reflection rooted in the very early days of the Church, the one that still underpins our experiences of faith seeking understanding.

The Universe Story brings us to another key moment in the history of our Church. The findings of modern science are well beyond what believers living in first-century Palestine could have imagined. The cosmology operative in the ancient Hebrew world depicted Earth at the center of creation with pillars supporting a heavenly realm of perfection that was the dwelling place of God, a cosmology that was geocentric and anthropocentric and had its roots in the Paleolithic era. For the ancient world, creation was a completed event, the cosmos was static and unchanging, the flat Earth motionless. Heaven and Earth were distinctly different realms, with heaven being the realm of the perfect and Earth the realm of the imperfect. We have seen illustrations that flow out of this cosmology, with God the patriarchal father seated on a throne, scepter in hand, looking down on the face of Earth. Although we have known for centuries that this cosmology is inaccurate, it is nevertheless the cosmology operative when our scriptures were written, and therefore operative in the language and images still used in our liturgies today.

Just as the early disciples allowed their own shaping and fashioning of the morphogenic field of early Christianity to evolve, just as they were unafraid to pose big questions and await the revelation of new wisdom that came through the working of the Spirit, we must engage the questions that the Universe Story implies. While the response of the disciples in the early dispute appeared to diverge from tradition, while something radically new emerged, it was nevertheless rooted in what had gone before and was therefore part of a continuous developmental flow. The message of Jesus himself, though rooted firmly in Jewish tradition, was in many ways a radical departure from what had come before. Throughout Christian history there have been moments of divergence in which a greater awareness or consciousness of the Spirit was made known. That is our tradition.

The Theology of Karl Rahner

What about modern theology? What has been the theological response to the Universe Story in recent times? Such a response comes from the work of Karl Rahner (1904–1984). A Jesuit and preeminent theologian of the Second Vatican Council, Rahner helped bring Catholic Christian theology into the modern world. Writing in an era when the Church had condemned modernism, Rahner was unafraid to pose questions about the compatibility of Christianity with an evolutionary view of the world and to ask whether modern thought had made Christianity obsolete. Aware of developments in science, he sought to integrate the notion of an evolving universe, which he acknowledged as "a given," with the central tenets of Christian faith.

In this section I want to capture the essence of Rahner's thought as it applies to our discussion of the Universe Story and the Christian story. I use many quotes because I want to draw directly from his own words, so as to demonstrate as carefully as I can how his theology is resonant with the Universe Story.

Rahner says that we live in a world of grace, that we are surrounded, shaped, and constituted by grace, which he defines as holy mystery's self-communication or self-offering in love. God creates in order to give God's self away. God creates in order to love. And grace is a universal phenomenon, not simply something granted to those who assent to particular beliefs. It is in the context of grace that Rahner offers his reflection on an evolutionary view of the world.

Rahner's discussion of Christian theology in light of evolution is rooted in the acknowledgement of one God. There is a single Creator of the entire cosmos, a Creator who remains present to every part of the cosmos, sustaining and empowering its ongoing life and development. This same Creator will bring the whole movement of evolutionary creation to completion. Such a holistic view of creation allows us to see the unity of spirit and matter. Responding to a world view that saw spirit and matter as distinctly different, a world view that eschewed the notion of spirit or anything for which there was no empirical evidence, Rahner sought to show how they were connected.

What is matter? Rahner says that it is the condition that allows us to experience the "other" immediately in time and space. "Matter is the ground of givenness of the other as the material of freedom, and the ground of real communication between finite spirits and mutual knowledge and love."[1] Denis Edwards explains further. According to Edwards, matter is:

> that side of ourselves and others which we experience as specific, concrete and bodily. We experience both ourselves and the world around us as matter insofar as both our own selves and the world around us appear to be factual realities, with their own proper and independent existence.[2]

As matter, we are atoms and molecules and cells, biological creatures that have evolved over deep time. The evolution of our material world began with the Big Bang, more than thirteen billion years ago. Ten billion years ago the first stars and galaxies appeared. Four-and-a-half billion years ago our Sun was born, and a half-billion years after that our solar system, followed by the emergence of Earth. Plant life emerged a little less than four billion years ago. As the evolution of the material world continued, animal life proliferated, with mammals emerging about sixty-five million years ago. About seven million years ago the first bipedal creatures evolved, followed by hominids. Our ancestors diverged from the great apes five to two million years ago. *Homo erectus*, thought to be the first to run, make fire, use tools, hunt consistently, and possibly use language, emerged nearly two million years ago. Ancient *homo sapiens*, our immediate ancestors, surfaced about a half-million years ago. The entire history of creation is characterized by evolution of matter, the process by which life becomes ever more conscious. This capacity to become more is what Rahner calls "active self-transcendence," and it is characteristic of all creation, not just the human. Incomprehensible holy mystery manifests as a continuous creative presence in the cosmos, enabling transcendence to occur because each created reality has within itself the potential to evolve into something more. But with the evolution of the human, a quantum leap of consciousness occurred. Grounded in biological evolution, we are material creatures who have come to an awareness of both our materiality and our otherness. Besides being material beings, we are also spirit.

What does it mean to be spirit? Rahner says that the experience is two-fold: spirit is the single person, conscious of and present to the self while having a sense of the absolute reality or mystery at the heart of life. There is a reciprocal relationship at work between these two aspects of human experience. We have an awareness of ourselves as separate entities—we experience our autonomy. Yet we know that this experience does not occur in a vacuum but is set in a larger context of unknown and unexpressed possibilities. This experience of spirit is not something that we possess. It is more like being possessed. To experience spirit is to recognize that our being is part of a process—one that is drawn into infinite mystery. Rahner says:

> It is only in the loving acceptance of this mystery and in its unpredictable disposal of us that we can genuinely undergo this process, and undergo it in that freedom which is necessarily given with transcendence of every individual thing and of one's own self. Insofar as the single person experiences himself in this way, he can and has to say: I am spirit.[3]

To be spirit is to be aware and awake to ourselves, and in that experience we become aware and awake to the sense that we are contingent beings possessed by a mystery that is "the absolute totality of all possible reality."[4] As we orient our lives toward this mystery, we exercise our freedom, the capacity that makes possible our transcendence.

Just as the material world has evolved, so has the spiritual. Rooted in the material realm, it is an aspect of human experience that has grown in complexity and consciousness. With the emergence of the capacity for self-reflection, there came an awareness of the transcendent dimension of reality. Through ancient *homo sapiens* came the rudimentary recognition that the self is contingent and that there is a dimension of human experience that lies beyond the material. Experiences of the transcendent dimension, of what we call the Holy, have always been received and then communicated from within the level of consciousness that the human has attained. Early on, our experience of the transcendent was connected to forces in the natural world, like thunder or rain, sun or moon. As we grew in our capacity to reflect, we recognized that the Holy was not to be identified with any particular thing and that it was an incomprehensible mystery that was far beyond our capacity to hold or control. The history of our faith can be viewed as the history of our growing recognition of who we are in relation to the sacred dimension of all reality. As we evolve, as our consciousness grows, so does our understanding of the ground of our being, that which we call God.

The capacities that allow human beings to apprehend the transcendent dimension of experience are what Rahner calls "existentials." They are at the heart of what it means to be human. It is human to want to know, to quest after the truth. Each response to a question becomes the ground from which we ask the next and the one after that. Our seeking after truth and our ever-growing capacity to hold what we have learned is an essential component of our being human. We also have the power to love, and that capacity expands as we mature. As we grow and develop, we are able to embrace more and more of life itself. We include more people in our circle of care and concern. Finally, the quest to know and the capacity to love happen within the context of freedom, our ability to see options, reflect upon consequences, and make choices that enable us to choose what is life-giving.

It is through understanding the fundamental unity of the material and spiritual dimensions of the human person that we can understand the unity of all created things. Rahner writes, "The Christian professes in his faith that all things, heaven and earth, the realm of the material and of the spiritual, are the creation of one and the same God."[5] If everything that exists has its origins in the one God, he asserts, then diversity proceeds from the one cause, the Creator. Variety exists, but since there is unity in origin, there is a single world:

> It follows from this that it would be unchristian to understand matter and spirit as merely existing alongside

each other in fact, and as being basically and absolutely disparate realities in relationship to each other. For
Christian theology and philosophy it is to be taken for
granted that spirit and matter have more in common
than they have differentiating them.[6]

According to Christian teaching, the human person is
not a contradictory or provisional composite of spirit and
matter, "but is a unity which is both logically and really ante-
cedent to the differentiation and distinction of its elements."[7]
In other words, spirit and matter are elements within a single
person that are a unity prior to their differentiation. There is
a fundamental wholeness and integrity to the human person
that cannot be thought of as separate or divided. "From this
perspective," Rahner continues, "it is clear that it is ultimately only from the single person and therefore only from
his or her single self-realization that we know what spirit and
matter are, and hence both must be understood as related to
each other to begin with."[8]

In Rahner's view matter and spirit are not haphazard elements without direction.

> . . . if the world is one, and if as one it has a history,
> and if in this one world not everything is already there
> from the beginning precisely because it is in the process
> of becoming, then there is no reason to deny that mat-
> ter should have developed towards life and towards [the
> human].[9]

The development toward the human is the development
toward spirit. Spirit is the goal of nature, and nature finds
itself in spirit. The cosmos becomes aware of itself in the
human, and thus "in the individual person and in the action
and activity of the human race" we find the "recapitulating
self-presence of the whole or of the cosmos."[10] In the human

being, the universe—the material world itself—comes to consciousness.

Rahner explains that it is the capacity for "active self-transcendence," present at every level of creation, that enables the material/spiritual human to continue to evolve. This capacity is "the essential foundation of the person, of responsibility, of religious experience (including mysticism), and of the possibility of God's self-communication in grace and revelation."[11] Self-transcendence is the presence of the incomprehensible holy mystery within the creature, pressuring it to become more. It is clear in Rahner's thought that the creature does not passively evolve through the intervention of any external deity, rather:

> . . . by producing the creature God endows it with the power of self-fulfillment and the conditions necessary to that end, so that it is not to be assumed that God will himself produce what can be achieved by the immanent development of the creature.[12]

The power of self-fulfillment, for self-preservation or *autopoiesis*—characteristic of every holon—bears witness to the presence of incomprehensible holy mystery working from within the creature, pressuring it to evolve. Thus the human person is fashioned to participate in its continued emergence as spirit. Not only have we become spirit, but we are made to continue to evolve in our manifestation of spirit, growing more aware of our spirit nature as we develop over time.

We have the capacity to respond to the dynamic impulse within us—holy mystery itself—as we live and move and have our being. As we grow in freedom and love, we begin to see that our acknowledgement of and participation in the spiritual dimension of life is an essential ingredient in the evolution of life itself. In this sense we are co-creators, our spirits evolving individually and collectively in a way that helps give shape to the material world. We live in a world of universally bestowed grace and are invited to participate in cosmogenesis, the ongoing evolution of a universe created through God's self-communication, which is love.

The movement toward consciously receiving God's self-communication takes place within the context of freedom. God's self-communication "can take place only in a *free* acceptance by free subjects."[13] While grace is always present, we must choose to activate its power by the choices we make. As we transcend, as we become more than we presently are, as we become more conscious and awaken to divine revelation, as we accept God's self-communication to us in our lives, we participate in the evolution of the cosmos.

The Incarnation

What about Jesus Christ? How does the Incarnation fit into an evolutionary theology? Rahner writes: "The God-Man is the initial beginning and the definitive triumph of the movement of the world's self-transcendence into absolute closeness to the mystery of God."[14] It is clear in Rahner's teaching that the experience of the Incarnation is not a break with evolutionary history, not an event standing outside of space-time, but a natural development in the universal bestowal of grace that leads to humankind's conscious acceptance of God's self-communication. It is essential that the Incarnation, embodied in the person of Jesus, is part of the entire experience of God's self-communication to the world. "He cannot simply be God himself as acting in the world, but must be part of the cosmos, a moment within its history, and indeed at its climax."[15] Jesus, then, must be "truly [human], truly a part of the earth, truly a moment in this world's biological process of becoming, a moment in [humanity's] natural history."[16] He is a human person "who just like us receives in his spiritual, human, and finite subjectivity the self-communication of God in grace."[17] Rather than a divine intervention into human history, the Incarnation is the inevitable result of the evolutionary process, of matter evolving toward spirit from the very beginning.

In the year 451 the Council of Chalcedon asserted that Jesus Christ is "consubstantial" with God and humanity. There is one Christ with two natures, human and divine. As human, Jesus was part of biological and historical evolution in the same way we are. But how do we understand him to be divine? Rahner says that "it is perfectly legitimate to employ the notion of an event through which [God's] self-communication and acceptance reaches a point in history which is irrevocable and irreversible."[18] This breakthrough occurred with and in Jesus, in whom God's self-communication and human acceptance become absolute, irrevocable, and irreversible. In Jesus "a human reality belongs absolutely to God," and the belonging is so complete that in the experience God's self-communication "is not only established by God, but it is God himself."[19] Hence, we maintain that Christ is divine. The offer of God's grace and the acceptance of that grace become a single movement, and in that experience we claim the two natures of Jesus Christ. It is in Jesus that "a human reality belongs absolutely to God."[20] Denis Edwards writes:

> Here we find an irrevocable unity between the one who offers and what is offered, between the proclaimer and what is proclaimed. In Jesus there is such a union between a human reality and God that we can say that this human proclamation and offer is a reality of God.[21]

Thus in Jesus we have a complete unity between God's offer of grace and humanity's acceptance of that offer. In this way Jesus is both the experience of the fullness of God and the fullness of humanity. Both realities converge and unite in this human person.

The Incarnation is a definitive moment in God's ongoing bestowal of grace on the entire world. It was a breakthrough, but not a break with the past. Rahner says that evolution of matter to spirit to Incarnation had already begun long before; "indeed it can be coexistent with the whole spiritual history of the human race and of the world, and this in fact is the case according to Christian teaching."[22] Jürgen Moltmann points out that "Jesus' history as the Christ does not begin with Jesus himself. It begins with the *ruach*/the Holy Spirit."[23] So creation and Incarnation go hand in hand, Incarnation dependent upon a created material world, the created material world fulfilled in Incarnation.

With the Incarnation, the entire world—not only humans or Christians—moves toward fulfillment. In this final phase, which Rahner points out is not necessarily its shortest, the world is "to realize its definitive concentration, its definitive climax and its radical closeness to the absolute mystery which we call God. From this perspective the Incarnation appears as the necessary and permanent beginning of the divinization of the world as a whole."[24] Raimon Panikkar states, "Jesus is the Christ, but Christ cannot be identified completely with Jesus of Nazareth."[25] Christ is a reality beyond the historical person of Jesus. In his last conversation with his friends, Jesus speaks to them: "Truly, truly, I say to you, he who believes in me will also do the works that I do; and greater works than these will he do, because I go to the Father" (Jn 14:12).

After Jesus' ascension the Spirit came—a fuller revelation of the same Spirit that had been present and pressuring all along—and we know that the Spirit enabled the followers of Jesus to become doers of great works. While Jesus was the evolutionary first, those who follow after him must enter into the process of accepting as fully as they can the divine self-communication that is at the heart of evolutionary history and human life. In this sense "the Christ" is not a reference to a person, but to a kind of consciousness that is resonant with the Spirit and expresses itself in freedom and love.

The empowerment to Christ consciousness came through the experience we refer to as the resurrection. While we cannot know precisely what happened, we know that the resurrection was more than the resuscitation of a corpse, as in the story of Lazarus. What we do know is that somehow the risen Christ made himself known to those whom he had called friends, and from this new way of knowing Jesus this formerly fear-filled band of followers became bold and wise.

In some way the resurrection revealed the identity of the one who had received God's offer in its fullness. Jesus, his followers came to know, was God enfleshed, and God now wanted to be enfleshed in them. Resurrection changed their consciousness in every way, and the world has never been the same. Humankind finally awakened to the recognition that through the presence of the risen Christ in us—the work of the Spirit in us—we are all now offered the possibility of being Christ in the world. All of us are invited and empowered to manifest this consciousness in the here and now, just as Jesus did.

Salvation

For Rahner, creation and Incarnation are two interconnected dimensions of God's self-communication to the world. In regard to the purpose of the Incarnation, from the early days of Christianity there have been two schools of thought. The first is that Jesus came to redeem us from our sin. The second is that the Incarnation was part of the divine plan all along and would have occurred even if there were no sin. Following theologians such as Bonaventure and Duns Scotus, Rahner rejects the notion that the primary purpose of the Incarnation is redemption from sin. (He does not deny sin but does not consider it the chief reason for the Incarnation.) For Rahner, the Incarnation has more of a collective, communal nature. He states that if we consider evolution as having any ultimate and one-way direction at all, then the process by which the universe becomes conscious of itself in the human must have a final result.

> In Christian terminology we usually call it [humanity's] final and definitive state, his salvation, the immortality of the soul or the resurrection of the flesh, but in doing so we have to see clearly that, when correctly understood, all of these terms are describing a final and definitive state of fulfillment for the cosmos.[26]

Salvation, then, in its fullest sense, is not about "me" or a very small "we," but about the cosmos as a whole. It is about the entire cosmos in some mystery-filled way coming to an awareness of its own divinity in divinity. "The clarity and finality of Christian truth lies in the inexorability of [humanity's] deliverance into this mystery."[27]

Christians acknowledge that our entry into the experience of salvation is through the paschal mystery, that is, through our participation in the death and resurrection of Jesus. If we consider Jesus as the embodiment of God's self-communication to humanity and humanity's acceptance of that self-communication, then the purpose of the Incarnation cannot be viewed as solely for the expiation of human sin, God's punishment leveled for our rejection of God's messenger.

Rather, this pivotal moment in human history embodied in Jesus is the result of the ongoing revelation of God and the ongoing reception by humanity. Jesus' death is not the act of a vengeful God. Elizabeth Johnson writes:

> To say that God willed Jesus to suffer makes God less good than a normal human being would be. Historically speaking, Jesus was condemned to death unjustly, a victim of human sinfulness and rejection. To say God handed him over is to blame God for what should be laid at the doorstep of human injustice. Rather, God wills life and not death, joy and not suffering, both for Jesus and for everyone else.[28]

The understanding that redemption is necessary because humanity had a fall from God's grace does not make sense in an evolutionary context. If all the life that we know began with the Big Bang, and we have been part of an evolution of increasing complexity and consciousness for 13.7 billion years, there is no former Paradise to which we may return. Jesus' death is not about a return to the past, but a promise for the future—a future of harmony in which all creation will realize its unity in the love of the divine.

Summary

This chapter has tried to identify some of the major ways in which the morphogenic field of Christian theology resonates with the morphogenic field of the Universe Story. We have looked at how theology is done, that theological reflection itself evolves as new questions arise that require the engagement of matters unheard of by previous generations. This ongoing process of discussion and dialogue is deeply rooted in our tradition, and our current grappling with issues resonates with how our tradition has responded throughout the course of Christianity. We will continue to experience resonance as we appeal to scripture and our experience of the Holy Spirit, yet we must be awake, knowing that it is the nature of the Spirit to do something new, to surprise us with insights that draw us to a new place in our relationships with God and others. The Universe Story has brought us to another Acts 15 moment in Christianity, and to remain relevant we must give the new questions careful thought and open discussion.

Karl Rahner's theology gives us a firm foundation from which to pose the questions that continue to arise. Grounded in human experience, Rahner's work reflects thoughtful dialogue with the discoveries of science from which the Universe Story has emerged. With a grasp of the process of evolution, he begins weaving the two stories together for us. Beginning with the notion that we live in a world of grace, Rahner looks at evolution from that perspective. The whole of creation can be seen as a single movement, the one grace-filled self-communicating act of the God who can only be described as incomprehensible holy mystery. From the beginning God's intention has been to work through the evolution of the cosmos in such a way that creation itself comes to consciousness. Rooted in matter, creation has always evolved toward spirit, and in and through the human being—the universe coming to consciousness—spirit recognizes itself.

The recognition and acceptance of spirit manifests most fully in the Incarnation. In the person of Jesus, the representative human, our species accepts in a definitive way who we are in God and who God is in us. Thus the Incarnation is not primarily about redemption from sin, but about coming to recognize our true nature.

The evolution of creation proceeds through what Rahner calls active self-transcendence—the presence of the Holy

Spirit within each creature pressuring it to evolve. Human self-transcendence operates only within the context of freedom, the capacity for which Christ set us free. As we continue to evolve, as we continue to awaken to our capacity for freedom, we continue to recognize the invitation to co-creativity that is implicit in our lives. Incomprehensible holy mystery asks us to participate in the ongoing unfolding of grace itself. The scientific discoveries that underpin the Universe Story make clear why our conscious participation is so necessary. All creation is an interconnected web of relationships.

The Universe Story and the Christian story resonate, to be sure. Each uses different language, but both point to a single reality—that there is the one creation from which all life comes. The morphogenic fields that these stories represent are strong and vibrant, and each holds essential elements that are part of the emerging Field of Compassion.

A CONTEMPLATIVE PAUSE

Settle into a quiet inner space, take a few deep relaxing breaths, and then, when you are ready, enter into the following exercises.

- I consider insights within me that have come throughout this chapter. Where is there resonance? Where is there resistance? Where is the realignment?

- I consider my own image of God, and who Jesus is, as well as how I connect with Spirit. Have these images evolved over the years? How do I name these experiences of the holy? What is newly emerging?

- I consider that I live in a world of grace—that I am surrounded, shaped, and constituted by grace. What evidence allows me to become more aware of grace?

A PRAYER

Holy One, evidence of your self-communication in love is all around, everywhere. In the inner depths of my own heart, in the world, in all creatures around me, you live and move and have your being. I am not separate from you, and because of your wondrous love I am not separate from all creation. Help me to live with eyes wide open to your self-communication. Help me to be open to your lavish grace, to receive it without fear and with the conviction that you want nothing more than for me to receive it. In turn, may I be gracious to others, an instrument of your lavish grace to all I meet. Amen.

chapter
four

Morphic Resonance: Two Stories Converge

The new cosmic story emerging into human awareness overwhelms all previous conceptions of the Universe for the simple reason that it draws them all into its comprehensive fullness. Who can learn what this means and remain calm?

Brian Swimme

The consciousness we possess as human beings, contrary to being a special endowment with which we seek to lord it over the rest of creation, needs to be freshly understood as an integral dimension of the "intelligence" that permeates all life in the universe. We belong to a reality greater than ourselves, an envelope of consciousness informing our awareness, intuition and imagination—in what is essentially an intelligent universe. All our thoughts, dreams and aspirations arise from this cosmic wellspring within which we live and grow, and are empowered to realize our full potential as planetary, cosmic creatures. Anything short of

*this global engagement leaves us unfulfilled, frustrated and
ultimately alienated from God and humanity.*

Diarmuid O'Murchu

Any newly emerging morphogenic field is rooted in and
resonates with morphogenic fields of the past. In chapter 3 we looked at some of the elements of the morphogenic
field of the Christian tradition that resonate with what is
emerging. It is important to acknowledge that there are multiple theologies within any religious system, each a different
lens through which human experience of the sacred may
be understood. The discussion of theology in the previous
chapter has been intentionally selective, for its purpose is
simply to show that integration of the Universe Story does
not require a rejection of the Christian story, and that the
two have many places where one illumines the other.

We have also noted that theology, as a morphogenic field
or holon, grows and develops over time. It dialogues with
other disciplines and new information. The church council in Jerusalem described in Acts 15 is an example of how
theological reflection occurs. The experience there was one
of many re-workings of what it means to be Christian, of
dialoguing with new information and allowing new understanding to emerge.

What is new is rooted in the past and has continuity
with it even as it breaks new ground. Ken Wilber uses the
principles "transcend and include" and "negate and preserve"
to describe this part of the process. When something novel
comes about, it is said to transcend the former expression,
yet that former expression is included in what emerges. We
have new insights about ourselves, for example, but the new
insight evolved from the former way of being and knowing
oneself. Even if the insight appears "from out of the blue," it

is our current ever-evolving experience that has enabled us to recognize and hold the new. We transcend the old, but it is still part of our experience, still included.

Another way to describe what happens is to say that we "negate and preserve" as we move to the new. When a child learns to walk, she negates crawling as her primary means of locomotion, yet in her experience retains the ability to crawl. She negates yet preserves. "Transcend and include" and "negate and preserve" are ways to say that each holon that emerges is nested in the old while the new holon or morphogenic field continues to evolve. This process is implicit in Acts 15 specifically and in Christian theology in general.

The Universe Story tells us that there is a single creation event that began more than thirteen billion years ago and continues in an ongoing process known as cosmogenesis. We know that the material world develops in the direction of greater complexity and greater consciousness. The Christian story has named that which brings about and maintains this creative process "God." Theology long ago rejected a deity that was simply a human, only bigger. God, as Rahner said, is incomprehensible holy mystery, the ground of all being, that which has created a universe that is made to evolve. In the process of evolution, there has been an increasingly fuller awareness of God's self-communication and its significance in human life and the life of all creation. And while we relate to the holy in and through our human experience, God is much more than we can ever hold in and through our human experience alone. Scientists tell us that the universe consists primarily of Dark Energy and Dark Matter. The vast majority of the cosmos is in an invisible and unexpressed form, at this point its own "incomprehensible holy mystery." That cosmic mystery is not identified as God, yet it cannot be separated from God. The point is that the holy remains primarily a mystery that we may engage but not resolve.

In *Thank God for Evolution!* Michael Dowd introduces an image of God that may be helpful in this discussion. He suggests that we consider God as the largest holon that transcends and includes all other holons. However, as the ultimate nesting doll, it is the holon or field that is not a sub-set of something larger:

> God, from this perspective, can be understood as a legitimate proper name for the largest nesting doll: the One and Only Creative Reality that is not a subset of some larger, more comprehensive creative reality. God is that which sources and infuses everything, yet is also co-emergent with and indistinguishable from anything. There are, of course, innumerable ways one can speak about Ultimate Reality and theologize about God. But if "God" is not a rightful proper name for "the One and Only Creative Reality that transcends and includes all other creative realities," then what is?[1]

This image retains the transcendent element of God (God is not to be identified as any particular thing) while allowing us to image the incomprehensible holy mystery as that which is present to us, that which pressures all creation from within to evolve.

Another resonance between the Christian story and Universe Story comes with Rahner's assertion regarding the unity of matter and spirit. His theology echoes with the scientific understanding of the fundamental connectedness of all creation. All that is conscious, all that is self-reflective, all that is spiritual, finds its roots in the material world. Unity precedes and enables diversity. In scientific language, it all began with a bang. In theological language, it all began with a creator.

"Active self-transcendence" is key to Rahner's under-standing of the creation's movement toward the holy, a capacity intrinsic to each and every holon, according to its level of complexity. For humans, the capacity to become more than one presently is—the ability to learn and imagine and move toward fulfillment of a dream—these capacities are there, whether the language we use is scientific or spiritual. Paul's insight that all creation is groaning toward its final goal (Rom 8:22) is a beautiful image of cosmic evolution described by science.

Some scientists say that when we look at the intri-cacies and immensities involved in the unfolding of our universe in the particular way that it has formed, it is easy to conclude that there is some sort of intelligence under-pinning it all. I think that is what Rahner meant by God's self-communication—the grace that surrounds, shapes, and constitutes all that is. While God is not to be identified with the cosmos, neither can God be separated from it, because it is the very life of God that creates and maintains life, not as some interventionist deity now and again dabbling in the world, but as an immanent God, an intimate God who is also with us from within.

How may we connect Jesus with the Universe Story? In the evolutionary story of the universe, quantum leaps occur in which something strikingly new emerges. First there was nothing, and then the Big Bang. There were no galaxies, and then there were billions of them. On Earth, there was no life, then unicellular organisms emerged. There was no human life, but at one moment in time ancient homo sapiens appeared. Evolution, rooted in habits that provide stability, proceeds in quantum leaps.

We could view the life of Jesus in the same way. Rooted in the concrete history of the cosmos and in the Jewish religious tradition, his was a new consciousness that witnessed reality in a unique way. Although Jewish tradition had always spoken of Yahweh's love, Jesus seemed to have a unique lens with which to view that love, and with that, a unique capacity to receive that love. Although he could not have used our language, he had a sense of an evolutionary flow, that what he had been given was not only for him, not only about him, but for a dynamic way of living that embraces all of humanity as an organic whole, as part of one's very self. This was indeed a breakthrough, a quantum leap in human awareness of itself—in relationship to incomprehensible holy mystery. The fully human Jesus was a full participant in the evolutionary unfolding of the cosmos.

The next place where the Christian story and Universe Story resonate is in the capacity for communion. A capacity of every morphogenic field or holon is that of self-adaptation or communion. If all life is fundamentally connected, then we cannot be anything other than in relationship. Our autonomy serves our ability to relate, to commune with other subjects. We are who we are in relationship.

Salvation is a central image in the Christian story, one that can also resonate with the Universe Story. In Rahner's view, the universe has a purpose, a goal—"salvation." But he makes clear that the depth of this doctrine has to do with the coming into awareness of the whole cosmos of its relationship to God. Salvation can no longer be thought of in terms of what Raimon Panikkar calls "tribal Christianity." Salvation in this context is a more profound reality than we've been taught to think or imagine.

Rahner's view of salvation acknowledges the connectedness of all that is, that we are in this evolutionary venture together, all creation, and that what one of us does affects all the other wholes of which we are a part. Salvation, therefore, becomes ultimately communal, even though on the human level it requires personal transformation in order for that to transpire.

Salvation is usually discussed in conjunction with the topic of sin, so perhaps it is necessary to say a few words about "sin" as it relates to the Universe Story. In an evolutionary context the word "sin" can sometimes cause difficulty. As a spiritual director I have heard the word frequently linked to a view that sees humankind as fundamentally flawed and subsequently under God's constant scrutiny. This perspective suggests that we have somehow lost an amicable connection to the divine as a result of Adam and Eve's "fall" from grace and that we must continually seek to repair the breach if we are to live in relationship with God. What can follow is a kind of spirituality in which the person feels the need to earn or prove worthy of God's love. This view of sin is a bit skewed.

Often this view is connected to a misunderstanding of the term "original sin." Rahner points out that this doctrine is easily and often misunderstood. It seems that two distinct aspects of the notion of "sin" become fused and then confused in our understanding. The first aspect is that of personal sin. We are each responsible for how we use our freedom, a gift of grace that enables us to be open and respond to the Holy in our personal lives. In order to be authentically free, we must have the option to say "no" to grace. Personal sin is defined as a turning away from God, a deliberate choice to reject God's grace-filled invitation to life and love.[2]

For most of us, what we name as "personal sin" evolves. As we mature, our sensitivity sharpens, and a spirituality that may have begun as a list of "dos" and "don'ts" can move toward one that requires more finely tuned responses: "What is the life-giving choice in this situation?" "How am I to love here?" "What will enable me to be more open to the Holy?" Accepting responsibility for our personal choices and their consequences as we grow, the use of our capacity for freedom, requires increasing subtlety.

The second aspect that is often confused with personal responsibility dates back to our earliest ancestors. We live in a world deeply scarred by collective human sin. Whether intentional or accidental, as a species we have wounded and been wounded, and day in and day out we are affected by the cumulative sin of humanity. Choices available to us are predicated on much of what has gone before. Our taxes and tithes are used for unjust wars and shameful scandals. Our unbridled consumption impoverishes people we will never meet. Much of the time we participate unconsciously, ignorant of the impact of our actions. This is what is meant by the term "original sin"—the *human condition* into which each of us is born, a condition we share and by which we are all affected. Everywhere we are part of a web of connections that have negative as well as positive impact, often despite our best intentions. Theologian John Sachs says, ". . . as individual human beings, we can never escape the 'human condition' of the whole. Our freedom is not free. On our own we are not capable of loving the world and God as we ought."[3]

Sharing in the human condition, however, does not mean that the sin of Adam and Eve has been imputed to each of us. Rahner makes that clear:

> . . . "original sin" in no way means that the moral quality of the actions of the first person or persons is transmitted to us, whether this be through a juridical imputation by God or through some kind of biological heredity, however conceived.[4]

In other words, we are not personally accountable for the human condition. That sin is not imputed to us, and we are not required to make amends for "the fall." Nor does "original sin" mean that we have been born depraved. It is simply a term used to designate the condition into which each of us is born—constricted by the collective choices made before us and the subsequent energetic fields they sustain.

In an evolutionary context it is possible to retain the two aspects of what we call sin—the personal "no" to grace and the human condition ("original sin"). But in an evolutionary view, the image of the connectedness of all life renders simplistic designations and clear-cut labels inadequate. If all life is connected on the most fundamental of levels, then every personal thought or action has an effect on the whole. In this sense, what has been considered personal is also collective. On the other hand, because of the ubiquity of global communication, we see the impact of systems in which we both willingly and unwillingly participate. In this sense, the collective becomes personal as the individual recognizes the destruction caused by cumulative personal actions. In an evolutionary universe, we recognize all too painfully that the collective and personal are one. Not excused from knowing or responding to what we witness, we are asked to allow a more mature notion of sin to emerge. An evolutionary point of view does not deny or contradict these two aspects of what we call sin. What it does reject is literal thinking that there was an Eden—a place on Earth in which human life was completely in conscious relationship with the Holy and to which we will return if we regain right relationship with God. In this context there is no paradise to recapture. Instead, we are on an evolutionary journey that invites us to become more and more conscious of the One who has graced us. As we grow in consciousness, we grow in unity with the divine grace that has brought us forth.

What if we considered "the fall" to be a touchstone that marks a fundamental shift in human consciousness? With every evolutionary advance there is a price to pay. Something breaks, then dies. The former way of living is no longer viable, and quite often there is the terrible realization that the comfortability of the past is forever lost. But in an evolutionary universe, while parts of the new are embedded in the past, devolution is not an option. We cannot go back. We cannot go back to slavery as an accepted social custom. We cannot go back to patriarchy that was once thought to be divinely ordained. We cannot go back to considering women as unclean during menstrual cycles or chattel to be bartered. Modern consciousness has not only evolved past such thinking, but it considers many previous ways of thinking and acting as unhealthy and harmful.

Today, in a global world, we can no longer be defined by tribal or ethnocentric consciousness. The "we" that once involved only our own clan has now evolved to include the whole of creation. Even as we are indebted to the old for its foundations that have enabled us to move to a new place, with each move into deeper consciousness there are aspects of the old that we reject because now we see what we could not see before. Letting go of what is no longer good or true, we bring the viable parts of the old into the future, hopefully in a form that is more fully conscious, more fully aware. And then even that will undergo change, and much of what we consider acceptable today will not be so tomorrow. As long as we continue to evolve, our understanding of what misses the mark will evolve, too.

The language we use to talk about salvation in connection with Jesus is a way we talk about entering into a mystery that makes sense of suffering and death. Jesus suffered and died, just like us. Jesus suffered and died for us, "for our salvation." In truth, suffering and death never "make sense," but they can be viewed from various perspectives, some of which are more helpful than others. Could we consider that the paschal mystery—the suffering, death, and resurrection of Jesus—is intended in this particular context to bring us to a kind of universal consciousness? The paschal mystery takes us from a narrow focus shrouded in our own pain and to a universal view. It does not discount our personal pain, but it brings us to the "big story," the one that underpins all others. As we enter into the perspective of the universal story, we see that death has no ultimate finality. Our entering the story of Jesus' death and resurrection has the power to bring us to cosmic consciousness, awareness that all life is connected not only in the moment, but in the past and future as well. For Christians, Jesus takes us to the big picture, and from that perspective we see more clearly who we are in the mystery of life.

One of the most beautiful images brought to us by the Hubble space telescope is that of the supernova. Brilliant and explosively dynamic, a supernova is the death eruption of an old, worn-out star. Our own solar system, in fact, came from such a dying star. Suffering and death, it seems, are integral to evolution. We know that the suffering that results from our shadow sides, both individually and collectively, did not end with Jesus' salvific action. Personal sin is still part of our reality, and our shadow sides are still quite powerful. What changed is that through the paschal mystery we get a glimpse of the God-sized picture—and that enables us to reach a more mature consciousness.

We get to see that we are part of a mystery of cosmic proportions, and when we see that, when we choose to participate in something cosmic, then we are transformed. With awe and wonder we see the infinite love of incomprehensible holy mystery poured out on a finite world. We are released from fear of death, for we know now that death is not final, for in death itself there is the seed of new life. We know on some level that may or may not be conscious that the existentials that define us—our self-awareness, our continuous quest to know, our ever-growing capacity for love and freedom—find their source in this elegant mystery that is our home and our destiny. Salvation has to do with embracing the existential capacities and choosing to live in a way that evolves them. Salvation is not about escaping death, it is about coming to the awareness that death is another face of life. Seeing with cosmic-sized consciousness shows us that cosmogenesis is life-death-life-death-life-death, an endless cycle propelled by infinite love. And in that recognition we find release.

Additional Elements from the Christian Story

Allowing ourselves to experience the resonance between the Christian story and the Universe Story is helpful as we move to a clearer understanding of the emerging field of consciousness. While the Universe Story itself is grounded in empirical science, the Christian story is rooted in the experience of human subjects who have acquired self-reflective consciousness, and as a result have meaning-filled insights regarding a dimension of life that falls outside the parameters of empirical science. To conclude this chapter I would like to mention three pieces specifically from the Christian story that are significant elements of the new morphogenic field that is emerging.

The first piece surfaces as we look again at the church "council" in Jerusalem (Acts 15). What arises from the story is the importance of listening. The significance of dialogue and genuine discussion cannot be underestimated. Underpinning the dialogue that occurred, there seemed to be an awareness that the way of being with one another to which these disciples had given their lives was a work in progress. Quite serious in their effort to respond carefully, they were willing to grapple with questions that continued to arise as a result of their fidelity to Jesus' way.

The listening that characterized the disciples' meeting was a deep listening, a contemplative listening. At the heart of the discussion was their experience of the risen Christ and their commitment to live in that consciousness with others. Yet they remained in connection with their past wisdom, using what they had learned about relationship with the holy mystery as they moved into a new space. Their questions were rooted in their very human experience, and it is significant that they listened to the experience of each person involved to cull out the wisdom each had to offer. They asked questions fearlessly, discussed and debated passionately, sought the guidance of the Spirit faithfully, and listened to one another contemplatively. What seemed to motivate the process was the desire to pass on to others what they themselves had received, and so the decisions they made reflected the desire to facilitate the understanding and practice of following Jesus in a way that was life-giving.

A second piece of the Christian story that is significant has to do with the connectedness between matter and spirit. Rahner's assertion that matter and spirit have more in common than they do differentiating them is important. Much of the difficulty that we have in our world today comes from the way we have tried to separate matter and spirit.

The scientific world has separated the two, disregarding the possibility of transcendence in matter, with the result of the natural world considered nothing more than a utilitarian resource. In the religious world the separation allowed spirituality to divorce itself from the real world, to disdain the material world as irrelevant to the spiritual. Now we know this is a place where our culture needs healing. The perceived separation of spirit and matter has caused fragmentation and alienation. One the one hand, the denial of the transcendent left us with only the material, and that mindset led to materialism. On the other hand, the divorce of the spiritual world from the material left us with an egocentric spirituality, one that became self-absorbed in a quest for personal salvation while failing to see the bigger picture. Earth itself is now paying the price for our short-sightedness.

The third piece of the Christian story that is significant for living in the new morphogenic field has to do with the existentials, the essential characteristics of the human that Karl Rahner discussed in his work. Human beings are the cosmos come to consciousness, and in the evolutionary process capacities have emerged that not only define us but make possible our role in co-creativity. First, we are self-reflective. Not only do we know, but we know that we know. Next, we ask questions, and when we have a response to that question, we ask another and another, endlessly, never satiated because the quest to know is like the experience of journeying toward a horizon that forever recedes, no matter how far we have come. Also, we love. And our love seems to have no limits. Those of us with children know the immensity of love that comes into our lives with the firstborn. That love does not diminish when a second child comes. It seems that our capacity for love is another horizon, another experience in which our ability to hold it continues to expand with the experiences of our lives.

Finally, there is the existential of freedom. Our self-reflective quest to know and to love takes place in the milieu of freedom, which Rahner explains as "the power to decide about oneself and to actualize oneself."[5] Freedom is our capacity to seek meaning and stake our lives on what we have discovered. It is the existential that enables us to make choices that evolve us, and it is the Holy One's challenge to live responsibly and co-creatively.

Conclusion

There *is* morphic resonance between the Christian story and the Universe Story. Each provides a different lens for interpreting reality itself. Each is a story of cosmogenesis and connectedness. Each invites us out of a narrowly focused view of reality and into a place of awe and wonder, and each resonates with the new morphogenic field that is emerging, a field of consciousness that invites us to engage our self-reflective awareness, our quest for knowing, our love and our freedom on behalf of all life.

In the process of evolution, something new is always on the rise—not something identical, but something novel and unique, something that has never existed before. The new consciousness will not be identical to what has already emerged, even as it is deeply rooted in morphogenic fields that have set the stage for it. Evolution will take what has already come to its next level of holarchy, a quantum leap to the "bigger picture" of cosmic, unitive consciousness. But first, there is one more morphogenic field to examine, one that is fecund with possibility and contains key elements of the new field—what Jesus called "the Kingdom of Heaven."

A CONTEMPLATIVE PAUSE

Settle into a quiet inner space, take a few deep relaxing breaths, and then, when you are ready, enter into the following exercises.

- I consider insights within me that have come throughout this chapter. Where is there resonance? Where is there resistance? Where is the realignment?

- Does Michael Dowd's statement that God is the reality that transcends and includes all other realities work for me? In what way is the imaging liberating? Restrictive?

- What are the questions that surface in me as I hold both the Christian story and Universe Story?

A PRAYER

Incomprehensible Holy Mystery, you come to me in so many ways—through the Christian story, which speaks of your love for all creation; through the Universe Story that brings me to awe and wonder. Help me to live out of the "big picture," to see how my life and all that I am about has cosmic significance. Help me to grow in my capacity for self-reflection, to expand my awareness of the communion of which I am a part. Enable me to grow in freedom and in

love, that I may be the co-creator you have invited me to be.
Amen.

chapter
five

The "Kingdom of God"

As for humankind today the realization of the Kingdom of God here on earth has become a matter of survival or extinction.

Albert Schweitzer

The kingdom of God is not to be in another world but it is the old world transformed into a new one.

George Eldon Ladd

Never before have we had such an opportunity to construct for the whole human family new world order where justice and peace for all is not a mere dream or utopia, but a plausible reality.

John Fuellenbach

At the center of Jesus' teaching and preaching is the image of the "kingdom of God." To anyone who would listen, Jesus invited and challenged them to participate in the vision that motivated all that he did: "I must preach the good news of the kingdom of God to the other cities also; for I was sent for this purpose" (Lk 4:43). Later in his ministry, after he had chosen the twelve apostles, he sent them out "to preach the kingdom of God and to heal" (Lk 9:2). This vision was central not only to his own life and ministry, it was the vision that he sought to pass on to those who would carry on his great work.

It is apparent that the new way of living that Jesus had in mind was a "here-now" rather than a "here-after" vision. Far from being a theoretical ideal or having a far-away location, this was to be a present reality, rooted in earthly space-time. It had to do with real relationships with real people, an inclusivity that disregarded cultural and religious convention and embraced a new way of living in response to the incomprehensible holy mystery Jesus called "Father."

The purpose of this chapter is twofold. First, it intends to examine the "kingdom of God" as an image that can engage our imaginations and attract us at this particular moment in history. The second purpose is to look at the "kingdom of God" as a morphogenic field—one within the Christian morphogenic field—that has powerful energy to fuel the newly emerging field. Much has been spoken and written regarding the vision of the "kingdom of God" in the life and work of Jesus. In this chapter I am choosing to discuss this image in order to show its relevance for our particular exploration and its resonance with the Universe Story and the larger Christian story. I recognize the limitation of language, particularly the patriarchal issues associated with the word "kingdom." And yet I need a phrase to designate a particular morphogenic field that emerged around the first century CE and was expressed in the life and ministry of Jesus of Nazareth. While this morphogenic field has evolved since Jesus' time, and frequently we change the language to words like the "reign" or "realm" or "kin-dom" of God, here I am using "kingdom of God" historically, to designate the particular field that holds the heart of Jesus' message.

In the context of our discussion of fields, the "kingdom of God" preached by Jesus is one that has been transcended and included, part of the evolutionary process that flowed through Jesus as his consciousness evolved past his own roots, continuing with Jesus' followers who engaged new questions and sought to attend to the movement of the Spirit as they made their way. But what is transcended is also included, a necessary part of the whole. Using the phrase "kingdom of God" here is my way of indicating the "transcend and include" nature of the evolutionary development that has occurred within the Christian tradition. At the same time, the "kingdom of God" is a morphogenic field in which many are presently rooted. Its message remains viable, and its essential components are alive and well in the new field that is emerging. And so, while using "kingdom of God" to designate a field identified with a particular period of history, I also acknowledge its existence in present time as well. In reality all language is limited, and it is my hope that language will not become an issue here, but rather a reminder of the very evolutionary flow of life this work is meant to highlight.

God's "Kingdom"

The most prominent feature of the "kingdom" that Jesus proclaimed is that it belonged to God. Jesus never claimed it as his own. If it does belong to God, then a place to begin our exploration is with the image of God that comes to us through Jesus' experience. In the gospels Jesus calls God "Abba," "Father," a reference to the intimacy of the relationship he experienced with God, not God's gender. Throughout the gospels we see Jesus going off alone to pray, suggesting that what fueled his passion and helped him carry on his mission was his connection with the Holy One. His relationship with incomprehensible holy mystery was unique, to be sure, and it was very real. The Incarnation, as we have noted, was the manifestation in earthly space-time of God's self-communication to creation. Jesus' life was sustained by his connection to the Giver of Grace, who imbued him with a radically new consciousness.

The Aramaic word for the divine is "Alaha." In *The Hidden Gospel,* Neil Douglas-Klotz says that in the gospels whenever Jesus speaks the word "God," we can replace it with "Alaha," which can be translated as "Sacred Unity, Oneness, the All, the Ultimate Power/Potential, the One with no opposite."[1] This word is also related to the Hebrew "Elohim," which shares the same root, "El" or "Al." Douglas-Klotz says that this concept of the sacred as Unity is "beyond names, forms, ideas, symbols, and concepts,"[2] resonant with the image of incomprehensible holy mystery in Karl Rahner's theology. In this sense, a proper name for the "kingdom of God" could be "the kingdom of Unity."

It is possible to say that the kingdom of Unity belongs to Alaha, the incomprehensible holy mystery whose self-communication began with creation and continues in and through this moment in time. It is mediated to us through Jesus, the one in whom the fullness of God's revelation meets the fullness of human acceptance. As the mediator of this new consciousness, Jesus chose to empower others to acquire that consciousness themselves, and the medium through which the teaching and learning took place was within the lived reality of the "kingdom of God."

The "Kingdom of God" in Scripture

Nowhere in scripture do we find a precise definition of the "kingdom of God." Jesus preferred to describe the vision in terms of images and parables, stories that spoke to the whole person and exposed the narrow and limiting aspects of his listeners' customary mode of consciousness, all the while inviting them into something new. What we do know from scripture passages in which Jesus makes reference, the "kingdom of God" is not something that money can buy, for "it is easier for a camel to go through the eye of a needle than for a rich man to enter the kingdom of God" (Mt 19:24). "The kingdom of God" is not a birthright or a result of having the right ethnic or political connections. It is not the product of human effort. Rather, the kingdom of Unity comes as a gift from God.

This gift that has been given to the disciples (Mk 4:11) is one that requires a response. Jesus tells the story of a man who had two sons:

> "What do you think? A man had two sons; he went to the first and said, 'Son, go and work in the vineyard today.' He answered, 'I will not'; but later he changed his mind and went. The father went to the second and said the same; and he answered, 'I go, sir'; but he did not go. Which of the two did the will of his father?" They said, "The first." Jesus said to them, "Truly I tell you, the tax-collectors and the prostitutes are going into the kingdom of God ahead of you. For John came to you in the way of righteousness and you did not believe him, but the tax-collectors and the prostitutes believed him; and even after you saw it, you did not change your minds and believe him." (Mt 21:28–32)

It seems that living out of the new vision had to do with doing God's will, that is, with engaging the invitation to co-creativity, to participating in life in a way that acknowledged the vital connection with God.

We must receive this gift of God with openness and vulnerability: "Truly I say to you, whoever does not receive the 'kingdom of God' like a child shall not enter it" (Mk 10:15). Once received, the kindom of Unity must be cared for and nurtured. It is like the farmer who sows good seed (Mt 13:24), or like the seed itself—a grain of mustard seed, "the smallest of all the seeds on earth" that grows and becomes a tree in whose branches the birds of the air build their nests (Mk 1:31, Lk 13:19). The realm of incomprehensible holy mystery is like the leaven a woman adds to flour (Mt 13:33), a treasure hidden in a field (Mt 13:44), a diligent merchant who finds a pearl of great value (Mt 13:45–46), and a great net filled with an enormous fish catch (Mt 13:47).

When asked by the Pharisees when the new reality was coming, Jesus replied to them, "The kingdom of God is not coming with signs to be observed; nor will they say, 'Lo, here it is!' or 'There!' for behold, the kingdom of God is in the midst of you"(Lk 17:20–21). In Matthew's gospel, both John the Baptist and Jesus tell their listeners to "Repent, for the kingdom of heaven is at hand" (Mt 3:2; 4:17). The "kingdom of God" is here. The "kingdom of God" is now.

Characteristics of the "Kingdom of God"

If we accept that the kingdom of God is intended to be a present reality, one that is experienced in the here and now, not in an other-worldly location at some other time, what then are its characteristics? What do we observe or hear Jesus say that in some way puts flesh on this vision to which he gave his life? How can we translate our observations into a description that makes sense for our day?

The first observation is that it seems that the full reception of this gift of God requires effort on the part of the receivers. Beatrice Bruteau writes, "The kingdom of God is not something in the far future that is going suddenly to come down from heaven and settle on you and magically turn everything right. You yourselves are It. It's in you and among you; you have to do It or It will never come."[3] The doing of the kingdom, its manifestation here on earth, requires our active participation. This echoes Rahner's assertion that we do not assume that God will bring about "what can be achieved by the immanent development of the creature."[4] We must show up and participate.

It is in the earthly manifestation of the kingdom of God that the fullness of the Incarnation—as the place in history where divine communication and human acceptance meet—becomes a collective reality. The manifestation of this collective reality is the Christian's essential call. Jesus' mission is to become our own. We, too, must respond to God's self-offering, and as we respond, as we become co-creators, we participate in humanity's ongoing self-transcendence into God.

In the Gospel of Luke, the ministry of Jesus began after he had been filled with the Spirit as the result of his desert experience. After teaching in synagogues throughout Galilee, he returned to the synagogue in Nazareth, the place where he was raised. The passage states that:

> . . . he went to the synagogue on the Sabbath day, as was his custom. He stood up to read, and the scroll of the prophet Isaiah was given to him. He unrolled the scroll and found the place where it is written:

The Spirit of the Lord is upon me,
because he has anointed me
to bring good news to the poor.
He has sent me to proclaim
release to the captives
and recovery of sight to the blind,
to let the oppressed go free, to proclaim the year
of the Lord's favor.

And he rolled up the scroll, gave it back to the attendant, and sat down. The eyes of all in the synagogue were fixed on him. Then he began to say to them, "Today this scripture has been fulfilled in your hearing." (Lk 4:18–21)

It seems clear that Jesus knew from the very beginning what the kingdom of God was to be about. It was about release and recovery; it was about liberty from oppression and the thought that one can be estranged from God. This seemed to be Jesus' mission statement, and we can see it being realized in all that he was about, especially in the multitude of relationships for which he was ceaselessly criticized. He ate forbidden meals with tax collectors and women and all those considered riffraff by the customs of the day. He was not afraid to touch the untouchable and to cleanse the unclean. People were irresistibly drawn to him, and his healing energy provided a steady stream of hope and compassion for those who thirsted for the simplest of human needs. Encounters with hypocrisy filled him with anger, and the sight of suffering moved him to compassion.

The "kingdom of God" as we witness Jesus living it is about responsible and caring relationships, ones that come out of a bigger story than Jesus' listeners were accustomed to hearing. "What counts is people," writes John Fuellenbach. "[Jesus'] interpretive key is compassion and justice, not holiness and purity. Love is the heart of the Reign of God. By loving this way, Jesus himself creates a liberating lifestyle and exhibits a wonderful freedom to do good." In and through his easy way of being with people, Jesus modeled and fostered relationships based on respect and love, for that is what he himself had experienced in his relationship with incomprehensible holy mystery.

It is evident that relationship is the focal point of the kingdom. Laws are not the primary determinant of human behavior; customs and customary actions are not to be accepted without question; expectations rooted in an incomplete way of imaging reality—ones devoid of love—are not obligatory. What is necessary, however, is a relationship that flows out of love. Love of both neighbor (Mt 19:19) and enemy (Mt 5:44) is required. To love an enemy makes him or her the neighbor that we are to love as ourselves—love not "in the same way I love myself," but love because in the realm of incomprehensible holy mystery, the neighbor and I are one, "the neighbor *is* myself."

The presence of love is healing. That is why wherever Jesus walked and talked and met others with unconditional acceptance and love, lives changed. We see in Jesus' encounters with others not only restoration of physical health, but restoration of place—the return to the dignity of being a human person loved tangibly, but with a tangibility rooted in unfathomable Holy Love.

Of course the love Jesus expressed to strangers was also present in the relationships with those closest to him. It seemed too that even his close relationships fell outside usual expectations. In a culture in which family ties were essential to social structure and even to life itself, Jesus lived in a social network that did not exclude family, but did not assume family to be automatic participants in the kingdom

(Mt 12:48–49). Even family members have to be intentional, have to choose to enter and live in unity.

Living the "kingdom of God" is bound to be costly. It involves great personal risk, for the refusal to be bound by convention and swayed by customs is a dangerous place in which to stand. Indeed, it cost Jesus his life. It cost him his life, his personal life as day after day after day he sought to bring about a new form of consciousness. It cost him his life in its final moments, when the resistance to the new consciousness and the rejection of change mounted what it thought was a final assault. In the clash of cultures—Jewish and Roman—that was the milieu in which Jesus lived, it was not difficult to see the danger and the probable consequence of engaging the energy that was in control.

It is surely such an awareness that motivated much of Jesus' teaching about the kingdom. "For which of you, desiring to build a tower, does not first sit down and count the cost, whether he has enough to complete it?" (Lk 14:28). The invitation to enter the kingdom of God is freely given, but its acceptance must be freely received and consciously chosen. It is not intended to be a whim based on good feelings, but calculated, with a knowledge of the risk and an acceptance of the cost.

But being willing to pay the price is not enough, either. "Another said, 'I will follow you, Lord; but let me first say farewell to those at my home.' Jesus said to him, 'No one who puts his hand to the plow and looks back is fit for the kingdom of God'" (Lk 9:61–61). When we freely and consciously choose to enter the kingdom, we must do so without compromise and without the distraction of anything that is less than the kingdom of God. We must break our ties with social expectations and cultural norms. We must commit ourselves fully to thinking and speaking and acting in this new way, because the pull and tug of the old will always seek to sever us from the new.

It is clear that to even consider the invitation to enter the kingdom, there has to be an exercise of freedom. Early in his ministry Jesus issued the invitation to a new consciousness with these words: "Repent, for the kingdom of heaven is at hand" (Mt 4:17). To repent is to respond, to turn, to gaze toward something anew, to stand in a different place, to become reoriented completely and wholly to what one most deeply knows to be true. Responding consciously to the invitation to enter the "kingdom of God" is a requirement, for in the act of choosing, in counting the cost and putting the hand to the plow, our capacity for self-transcendence, rooted in freedom, activates. We become fully alive subjects rooted in relationship with the Holy One, who pressures us from within to evolve, who communicates to us in love and empowers us to manifest that love "on earth as it is in heaven."

The activation of self-transcendence is a key component of the kingdom. Jesus did not ask his listeners to have faith in him as much as he asked them to have faith in themselves— to trust that the divine life was not separate from their own. Neil Douglas-Klotz says that the word usually translated as "kingdom" is *malkuta* in Aramaic and *mamlaka* in Hebrew, the equivalent of the Greek *basileia*. (All three are feminine in gender, he points out, which means that the more accurate translation is "queendom.") The root of the word *malkuta* points to a fully formed extension of power "that is centralized and determined." *Malkuta* "is the sign of the creative word, the empowering vision, the counsel that rules by its ability to express the most obvious next step for a group. On a personal level, this root expresses that which says 'I can!' to life."[5]

Douglas-Klotz says that before there were queens or kings in the Middle East, most people were nomads who traveled and lived in clans. Clan leaders were most often those who "by their vision and wisdom could say 'I can' on behalf of their communities—for instance to guide them at the right times and to the right places to graze animals or gather food."[6]

Beatrice Bruteau points out that this kind of energy—We can!—is an important dimension of Jesus' vision and invitation.

> They believed that things could be improved, that people can change their attitudes and behaviors, that the deep meaning of life is goodness, generosity, caring, sharing, and happiness. The "kingdom of God" is the world in which such values prevail, and it is brought into being just as fast as people actually assent to those values and express them in their daily lives.[7]

In his run for the U.S. Presidency in 2008, Barack Obama used the campaign slogan, "Yes We Can," to activate the support of thousands of American citizens. The energy was palpable and seemed to inspire people to recapture a vision and move toward it in hope. Without discounting the difficulties, Obama tapped into the capacity of every holon to evolve, to become more than it presently is, to be truly free in the sense of becoming aware and responsible of what is within and around it. He was calling his listeners to self-transcendence on behalf of a nation.

This is the energy of *malkuta*. It is an energy that empowers, that releases us from whatever bondage that straps us, that releases us into the world with hope and the conviction that things can change. Nothing has to remain the same. Big dreams flowing from big stories are not phantasms disconnected from reality, but are the result of the divine dream already activated within us. To dream of love and compassion, justice and peace, to envision a way of living in which self-preservation and self-adaptation are fulfilled in the ongoing process of self-transcendence—this is no deluded fantasy. It is our call—a call that will take every ounce of our capacity for self-transcendence, every bit of our freedom to choose, every piece of a courageous commitment to the work that brings it forth. We dream of it, not because it is impossibly far away, but because it is within us. The "kingdom of God" is already within us, or we would be unable to imagine it. All that it takes to activate the dream and live it in the here and now is already within us. All that it takes is our knowing and intending that it can happen and our engaging others to walk with us. It may not happen overnight—but it could. All it takes is enough of us to hold the vision and to move forward as we say, "Yes we can!" *Malkuta* is within us.

The "Kingdom of God" as a Morphogenic Field

Like the Universe Story and the Christian story, the image of the "kingdom of God" is a morphogenic field—a non-material region of influence. The morphogenic field of the kingdom, though not bound by space and time, manifests tangibly in the material world. The field holds the particular kind of energy that is characteristic of the kingdom. Like any morphogenic field or holon, this one has evolved over time, while still retaining its characteristic elements. Through morphic resonance it sustains itself, sustains its members, and attracts those with similar resonances. And through morphic resonance it will influence the emergence of the new that transcends and includes this particular form.

The kingdom of God-morphogenic field is rooted in the life and ministry of Jesus, which is itself rooted in Jewish tradition. It has evolved as it has responded to changes in the world, yet it has maintained an identity over centuries, giving it viability, power, and sphere of influence that invite others in. While it is dynamic, it is stable and coherent in its energy.

Relationships are central to the kingdom of God-morphogenic field. It is a here-and-now actuality that is concerned with real relationships and real people. Relationships have value because they are connected to and flow out of the incomprehensible holy mystery that is the source of all life. While this particular morphogenic field is a gift, one must choose to enter it freely and with commitment, activating the capacity for self-transcendence that is the Holy One's spirit working within. It is costly and risky, requiring a turn from other ways of living and a full embrace of this one. While it is clear that the kingdom is the focus of the ministry of Jesus, it does not belong to him. Followers are to make it their own, to live it, to flesh it out, to give their all to it so that it becomes their identity—and a collective reality, which is the only way that love can become authentic.

With the kingdom of God-morphogenic field already resonant with hope and power, already included in what has emerged, we can begin to describe the new morphogenic field that is emerging in our day. The new field is part of the ongoing process of evolution of all holons. What is emerging transcends but includes the former, dependent on that which went before, but with an energy that distinguishes it from that which went before. In the next chapter we begin to look at relatively new pieces of human experience that have surfaced since Jesus first began to invite us to become the kingdom. These new pieces transcend what Jesus taught, in the sense that they are newly evolved powers that have emerged—perhaps the "greater works" that Jesus mentioned in John 14:12. Yet in their transcending they include the former, in some ways amplifying its essential truths while allowing that which is not of the essence to drop away.

A CONTEMPLATIVE PAUSE

Settle into a quiet inner space, take a few deep relaxing breaths, and then, when you are ready, enter into the following exercises.

- I consider insights within me that have come throughout this chapter. Where is there resonance? Where is there resistance? Where is the realignment?

- What element of the "kingdom of God" is the greatest challenge for me? Are there parts of it that I perceive as impossible to achieve?

- Where do I see the use of the four characteristics of holons (self-preservation, self-adaption, self-transcendence, self-dissolution) active in the kingdom?

A PRAYER

Holy One, for the longest time we have prayed, "Your kingdom come," and often we have wanted it to come in a supernatural way that did not ask too much of us. We have longed for your reign but imagined it elsewhere, not recognizing that it truly is a gift you have already given—but a gift that calls forth all our own gifts to receive it as fully as you intend. Let your kingdom come into our hearts and into our hands, and help us to activate it in our lives through the choices we make and the relationships we enter. May our own self-transcendence cause us to grow in freedom, and from the place of freedom may we choose to live in compassion and love. Amen.

chapter
six

Emerging Capacities

Behold, I am doing a new thing; now it springs forth, do you not perceive it?

Isaiah 43:19

Earth cannot be changed for the better unless the consciousness of individuals is changed first.

Declaration Toward a Global Ethic

When you get over yourself and you see beyond your own ego, you discover that who you are is not separate from the very impulse that is driving the creative process, and you begin to understand that as that impulse, you are definitely here for a reason!

Andrew Cohen

In an evolutionary universe something new is always happening. Scientifically speaking, for 13.7 billion years the cosmos has continued to expand and evolve in ever greater complexity and consciousness. Theologically speaking, God's self-communication, the bestowal of grace upon creation, has been integral to the evolution of the material world, and in the process our own species with its unique kind of reflective consciousness has grown in its capacity to receive God's self-communication and respond with greater awareness and depth. The Universe Story and the Christian story with the "kingdom of God" are three distinct fields that share morphic resonance. At root, each is a story/holon/morphogenic field that renders a picture of the cosmos as a unified whole with all its parts connected in an endless web of relationships. These relationships manifest in the material world—here and now.

One way to speak of the Christian story is to say that God is always doing something more. Incomprehensible holy mystery is always giving more, revealing more, communicating more. The only limit to that giving has been creation's capacity to receive. A look back over the history of creation suggests that as our species has continued to evolve, our capacity to recognize and respond to the holy has grown. Early on, at the dawn of human consciousness, we identified God with forces of nature outside ourselves. We imagined that gods had to be appeased so that the terrible natural catastrophes that threatened life could be averted or survived. As human consciousness grew, so did the capacity to notice and reflect upon the sacred impulse that seemed to be part of every tribe and culture that emerged. Each evolutionary move forward can be viewed as the next step in our ever-growing capacity to receive God's self-communication. Perhaps the greatest work for any generation is growth in the capacity to recognize where and how God is doing something new, and then to accept the challenge to respond to it and give it flesh.

It is important to remember that in an evolutionary universe nothing is ever complete beyond its own moment in time. In this context, God's self-communication is always "incomplete." It is always held back, in a sense, not because of God's lack of desire to give, but because we cannot possibly hold all that God has to offer—at least not collectively in this moment of our history. As we evolve and continue to become more conscious, whether individually or collectively, our capacity to receive deepens, so that we are able to hold more and more of the sacred self-offering. The emergence of the new does not invalidate what has gone before, but in a sense fulfills it, affirming its truth even as it draws the former manifestation into a fuller-still revelation of truth.

This means that we must always stand in a place that is paradoxical in its nature. We stand where the fullness of 13.7 billion years of evolution is manifest. Nothing has ever been this deeply known or revealed before. At the same time, what has emerged is incomplete. Its fullness is for today only, for tomorrow our capacity to hold truth is a little deeper and so the revelation we receive will be a bit fuller. In a way this can bring a sense of relief. In an evolutionary world, nothing— as full as it may be—is ever final. Any critical judgment we make will be with partial knowledge and therefore faulty. Everything is unfinished, its edges rough, its ultimate refinement lacking.

It would seem that fulfillment then cannot come from satisfying or accomplishing a goal that rings with finality. Fulfillment must come from the satisfaction of being the kind of human who is able to cooperate with God's self-communication in a way that is life-giving both to self and the world, to all the holons of which we are a part. Since we profess that God's ongoing revelation has to do with love, perhaps the measure we must use to gauge our own emergence has to be in our capacity to hold love, to allow ourselves to be conduits of love. That is the way we serve God and the world to which we owe so much. That is where we find personal fulfillment, for in learning to be one who lives in the embrace of love, we engage all the existential capacities that have evolved thus far.

We live in a unique moment of time. We do not know for certain whether our species will survive the current crises, but if we are to survive, we will have to do so from within a new consciousness, one that counters the notion that the universe is a meaningless machine of which we are merely disconnected parts. The new consciousness is a morphogenic field that arises out of the old, yet surpasses what has gone before. The Universe Story and the Christian story with its image of the "kingdom of God" are established morphogenic fields that make possible the new. The new field of consciousness does not invalidate what has gone before. It renders it more complete and keeps on evolving as ever more complete expressions emerge.

In our moment of time, some critical new awarenesses have emerged, ones that enable us to respond to the crises we face. If a new consciousness is what the Spirit is pressuring us to embrace, then the tools we need for that new consciousness will emerge. I have identified three emergent awarenesses and powers that I think enable us to participate more fully in the co-creative activity that is to be our work at the present time.

The first is the emergence of a level of consciousness that can be described as "unitive." Although exceptional individuals in human history have exhibited this level of consciousness before, now it is measurably present on a greater scale. By examining the work of Susanne Cook-Greuter, we will identify the characteristics of this stage of adult development and look at how it resonates with what is emerging.

Second, research is beginning to show the benefits of meditation as a way to access the inner wisdom that is crucial to acquiring the new consciousness. There are meditation practices that help create a balance between left- and right-brain activity, releasing creativity and helping facilitate the move to the new psychological level of development that has emerged.

Third, the study of intentionality—the practice of setting intentions and behaving in intentional ways—has also been a promising development. Our energy is powerful, to be sure, always affecting the relationships and quality of connectedness that fill our lives. To be able to direct our energy in constructive, life-giving ways is an essential element of the new morphogenic field. The remainder of this chapter will describe the first of these three emergences, unitive consciousness.

Unitive Consciousness

The first awareness that has surfaced is the recognition that a new level of adult development has emerged, with greater numbers of adults reaching this point than ever before. Throughout human history there have been individuals whose consciousness can be described as unitive consciousness—living in a way that expresses their experience of oneness with all that is—but it seems that now the number is increasing, as evidenced through empirical research. In her work at Harvard, Dr. Susanne Cook-Greuter, a student of both Robert Kegan and Jane Loevinger, has examined the higher stages of adult maturation known as postautonomous ego development. It is her work that forms the basis for this discussion of unitive consciousness.

Cook-Greuter has examined the latter stages of adult development and delineates more clearly some of the characteristics that have been grouped together in previous studies. Her research is based on data collected over ten years, enabling her to make finer distinctions among traits that are characteristic of the higher stages. The study also provides empirical evidence confirming that a larger number of adults are reaching postautonomous stages of development.

According to Cook-Greuter, "Human development in general can be looked at as a progression of different ways of making sense of reality."[1] One way to look at the progression through the stages is as the evolution of worldviews. Each worldview has its own characteristic mental model of the world, level of moral development, and way of making sense of reality. Cook-Greuter refers to the evolution through stages as levels of increasing embrace, with the subject acknowledging a growing sense of connectedness to ever larger wholes that occur as development proceeds. Like any morphogenic field, that of human development consists of successive levels of complexity, with each newly emerging order nested in the one below. Each step forward is accompanied by increased inclusivity, a more expansive view of personal and universal history, and increasing self-reflective awareness.

Cook-Greuter says that 80 percent of adults fall into the stage identified as "Conventional." She writes, "By most modern Western expectations, fully functional adults see and treat reality as something preexistent and external to themselves made up of permanent, well-defined objects that can be analyzed, investigated and controlled for our benefit."[2] This worldview is based on the notion of separation between subject and object, thinker and thought. Cook-Greuter states that most adults have little or no insight that the defining of objects is essentially arbitrary. "They operate under the assumption that subject and object are distinct, and that by analyzing the parts one can figure out the whole."[3] This, she asserts, tends to be the goal of socialization from the Western perspective and how that perspective defines the fully grown adult. But this perspective is far from complete.

The two stages that we will explore here lie beyond the Conventional phase. Postautonomous adult development looks at stages of growth in which the perception of the separation between subject and object are going or are gone. Reality is known to be more than an assembly of parts, and the ego, as "the underlying principle in personality organization that develops and generates coherent meaning throughout life,"[4] is recognized as limiting, as it renders an illusory picture of reality. In the postautonomous stages, rationality is no longer viewed as the only way to understand the world. Other ways of knowing are embraced, and the sense of being able to know everything and solve every problem, if only given enough time, gives way to a witnessing of a world in constant flux. Persons in these stages engage the world in a different way, with less fear and less need to control.

The two highest stages Cook-Greuter explores are of significance as we look at the new consciousness. She divides unitive consciousness, the highest stage she was able to examine empirically, into two separate stages. It is important to note that a person can be quite mature without attaining these final stages, but it is significant that we look at them because we find in their descriptions some of the characteristics that are called for as we live in the new morphogenic field. Normally these traits are characteristic of persons who have been long on the journey, who are mature in their outlook and interactions. They are highly functional and self-reflective. Whether or not they can name it as such, these individuals have been engaged in the process of self-transcendence and are fluent in the capacities that characterize each and every holon. They move comfortably between autonomy and communion, and are able to grapple with the experiences of self-dissolution in healthy ways. The stages we look at here presuppose and are nested in this maturity.

The first stage is what Cook-Greuter calls "Construct-Aware," and those in this phase "generally have a dynamic and multi-faceted understanding of human nature and the complexities of human interaction."[5] They live out of a stance known as the "witness," able to detach from their thoughts and behaviors, with the capacity to observe them. Construct-Aware individuals have begun to see the limits of their own egos, which they recognize as constructs—constructed reality, notions *about* reality, not reality itself. "Unlike earlier stages, Construct-Aware persons are aware of the ego's clever and vigilant machinations at self-preservation."[6] For the first time the person experiences the ego as transparent, and what accompanies this experience is the awareness of his or her own fundamental egocentricity. Cook-Greuter says, "Final knowledge about the self or anything else is seen as illusive and unattainable through effort and reason because all conscious thought, all cognition is recognized as constructed and, therefore, split off from the underlying, cohesive, non-dual truth."[7] All our thoughts, all that we think we know, the Construct-Aware adult learns, is illusory, a constructed reality assembled by the ego.

Construct-Aware adults turn inward and begin to witness their own attempts at meaning-making. They recognize that the limited ego has directed the meaning-making process and that what has been defined as real and meaningful has been based on illusion. What then emerges is the acknowledgment that nothing has intrinsic meaning, but meaning is assigned through the choices one makes. The person discovers that what lies outside oneself does not define the self nearly as much as what lies within. In this sense, the person can say "I make my own meaning." This is an entirely different worldview for the person. Now aware of the internal para-doxes and the limits of rational thought, Construct-Aware adults discover that the ego is simply a map of reality—and that "the map is not the territory."[8] This opens up entirely new possibilities in the way the person thinks about self and how the person interacts with the world.

The worldview of the Construct-Aware person is expan-sive. In a sense the person has a foot in two different worlds. The first is in the world that experiences the self as separate, as different from the world. However, the other foot has stepped into a place that recognizes that there is no separa-tion at all, that life is an endless flux of valleys and hills, births and deaths, joys and sorrows. The person now recognizes that much of what has been considered meaningful and true has been based on illusions that begin to melt away as this new way of perceiving reality takes hold.

Construct-Aware persons are also able to witness their emotional and rational processes and behavior. "They pay attention to the automatic judgment habit as well as the habits of mind such as our endless analyzing and reflecting in order to create ever more accurate theories of life and nature."[9] The person realizes "that the pursuit of objective self-identification and rational, objective explanations of the universe are futile—artifacts of our need to make permanent and substantive that which is in flux and immaterial."[10] At this phase the person also sees the limitations of language. While appreciating the function of words, the person rec-ognizes that "the language habit works to support the ego's supremacy" and contributes to the artificial constructs that support illusions.

Individuals at this stage are accustomed to turning inward and observing the self. Cook-Greuter says that this turning inward "often leads to the spontaneous experience of a direct mode of being in which knower and known momentarily merge, and the personal self-sense disappears."[11] In an experiential way the person begins to reside in the awareness of the connectedness of all that is. The sense of separation that was once part of the person's experience is now recognized as illusion. Part of what is happening in this stage of development is the relinquishment of the self as a separate identity, an identity that has been the result of a lifetime of effort and achievement. At this phase the person becomes aware of how attached he or she is to this separate sense of identity. Cook-Greuter writes:

> Even if we understand that letting go of our attachment to the known will bring freedom from familiar kinds of suffering, attempts at doing so are ineffective and often lead to intractable paradoxes. The more one becomes attached to the idea of non-attachment, the more firmly one remains fettered. The more one is conscious and proud of one's psychic powers and ego-transcending quest, the more clearly one's ego is still enthroned.[12]

Grappling with paradox is a hallmark of this postautonomous stage. Having recognized the ego's shenanigans, there is the recognition that life itself is filled with paradox, but whereas before paradoxes were seen as puzzles to be solved, they are now viewed as true expressions of the real, which need to be embraced and integrated. Essentially the Construct-Aware person becomes able to hold contradictions without judgment and the need to have them resolved.

It would seem obvious that the action of the Construct-Aware individual is quite different from those who are still governed by well-intentioned but ego-driven perceptions of reality. To those who are at the Conventional level or below, they can appear quite aloof because they are not engaged in the world in the same way as most others. Coming out of the stance of the witness, they have a very different awareness of what is going on and are not driven by fear. With a worldview that sees life as an endless flux of ups and downs, they do not panic but hold what is happening with a sense of peace. This is not to say that they are not engaged in the world, because in fact they have the power to be transformative agents in the world. The basic difference is that they are, for the most part, free from ego-driven agendas that, however well intentioned, often interfere with transformation. Construct-Aware adults know that at root, it is the quality of consciousness that determines all manifestations in the world.

Adults who evolve to this stage of consciousness can feel quite lonely, for in fact there are few others like them. Few others understand their perspective, for this is the first stage of adults that reflects upon their experience in terms of evolutionary change. At the same time, because they have mature insight into the nature of the human person, they "usually have superbly fine-tuned interpersonal skills and insight into others' complex and dynamic personalities and the space between people."[13] They are empathic listeners whose feedback can invite others to transformation.

To summarize, the Construct-Aware person lives out of the place of witness that is able to observe the self. The person at this stage recognizes the limits of ego and how the ego has been central in constructing meaning, as well as realizing that final knowledge about the self and the world cannot be attained. They also witness their emotional and mental habits, becoming aware that objective explanations are useless. They witness the limits of language, seeing that language, helpful as it can be, is also a human construct, not reality itself.

With a well-developed interior life, the Construct-Aware are used to turning inward and observing interior movements

with relative clarity. Often this inward turn leads to spontaneous experiences in which the knower and known become
one as the personal sense of the separate self disappears.
Those at this stage often deal with loneliness because so few
others have come to this place in which life itself is viewed
from an evolutionary perspective. Because they are able to
deal with their own egocentricity and illusions, they tend to
be humble people who grasp the big picture, who can act
without agenda, listen empathically, and respond sensitively
to those around them.

The Unitive

Those who continue postautonomous development reach
the second of the Unitive stages, what Cook-Greuter calls the
Unitive. At this stage the person shifts to a new worldview
or way of perceiving human existence and consciousness,
a perspective that can be described as universal or cosmic.
From this perspective individuals "experience themselves and
others as part of ongoing humanity, embedded in the creative
ground, fulfilling the destiny of evolution."[14] While at the
earlier Construct-Aware phase the person experiences the
self as separate, now "feelings of belongingness and feelings
of one's separateness and uniqueness are experienced without
undue tension as changing perceptions of many possibilities
of being."[15] Unitives are attached to neither belonging nor
not belonging, and this non-attachment is what allows them
to witness life with greater ease.

Unitives are able to see the vast array of human experience—the passing of ages, social, cultural, historical, as well
as their own personal history—from a witness perspective.
They can take multiple points of view and shift focus among
various states of awareness. They can hold the whole and the

details simultaneously. They feel embedded in the world, in nature itself. Birth and death, joy and pain are embraced as natural occurrences, "patterns of change in the flux of time."[16]

"Persons at the Unitive stage can see a world in a grain of sand, that is, they can perceive the concrete, limited, and temporal aspects of an entity simultaneously with its eternal and symbolic meaning,"[17] Cook-Greuter writes. They can notice the differences in others with respect, not needing anyone to be other than they are, not viewing higher stages as better than lower ones, because all are necessary parts of an inter-connected reality within an evolutionary process. Unitives accept both themselves and others "as is."

With a universal or cosmic perspective in which everything that happens is viewed as part of the flux of the evolutionary process, Unitives, like the Construct-Aware, can appear aloof because they are not involved in the usual pursuits that occupy others. Secure in themselves, their very presence and way of being in the world can challenge others as they live in a way that counters the rational, evaluative, conventional ideas that rule so many others. Cook-Greuter points out:

> In contrast to all other stages, Unitive individuals seem to have intense, non-demanding relationships with people regardless of their development, age, gender, or any other indentifications. Because they see the dignity in all manifestations of life, they can make others feel worthy and whole.[18]

The very presence of the Unitive invites others to transformation.

Unitives care very deeply about the human condition, seeing themselves embedded in the evolutionary process of the entire universe. Their sense of identity comes from this cosmic stance, and their life's work can be seen simultaneously as the expression of the unique self and as simply being part of shared humanity. Unitives "work for justice, fairness, and benevolence towards all. Though taking responsibility for meaning making, they don't perceive themselves to be the sole and lone masters of their souls."[19] Their moral stance is an internalized one, one that flows out of self-knowledge, knowledge of the human condition, and the sense of purpose and wholeness that is part of their world view. They know that their lives fulfill a cosmic purpose, a purpose that may be lived in simplicity and integrity. They recognize that "[d]oing and being are just modes of existing, but not intrinsically more valuable than feeling, being or non-being."[20] They get what Einstein meant when he said that the notion of separation is an "optical delusion" and can grasp the truth of the Buddhist precept: "Understanding is the ultimate illusion."

Like Construct-Aware individuals, the Unitives can embrace the contradictions, incongruities, and paradoxes of life with comfort, a stance we can see in the words of Richard Rohr: "The more I am with the Alone, the more I surrender to ambivalence, to happy contradictions and seeming inconsistencies in myself and almost everything else, including God, paradoxes don't scare me anymore."[21]

With the Unitive, the whole person—integrated—engages the world. The whole person engages the rational mind while acknowledging its limits. The whole person engages the emotions without being identified with them. The whole person lives out of the place of witness with non-attachment, but non-attachment does not mean non-engagement. The perception of duality has given way, and "either/or" thinking has given over to "both/and." What used to be viewed as terms in contradictions are now viewed without a sense of opposition. Life and death, success and failure, good and bad—all are seen within the larger context of non-duality in which all reality is one.

Unitives have nothing to prove, no ego to defend, no need to achieve anything or be anything other than in the present moment. They cherish difference and diversity, seeing every piece as a necessary part of a mystery-laden whole. Judgments and their accompanying "shoulds" have dropped, replaced by an acceptance and appreciation of all that is, no matter what the point of view or level of consciousness. It is as if they are able to hike from holon level to holon level, throughout the entire range of holarchy, capable of identifying and affirming each stage of life as vital to the whole. Bill Harris says:

> The Unitive sees happiness *and* unhappiness as part of the necessary, temporary (and endless) fluctuations inherent in the human situation. Instead of seeing life in a dualistic way, where some things are appropriate and desirable while others are inappropriate and undesirable, the Unitive experiences the world as a place where all opposites "arise together" and "go together. . . . The Unitive watches as positive turns to negative and back to positive, endlessly—and necessarily. [22]

At the same time, the person in this stage has access to the entire range of human experience. They have cosmic awareness while being able to apprehend detail. They have access to the full range of emotional expression and "can be personal or global, simple or complex, serene or active, rational or transcendent, sublime or silly."[23] Because they live in the moment, they are not caught up in past struggles or future fears, but can respond spontaneously as needs arise. With such broad scope of vision and non-attachment to people or things or outcomes, the often-intuitive Unitive can bring creative solutions to situations that call for a response.

Certainly this worldview differs from the conventional stance of our dominant culture.

To summarize, the Unitive's worldview is universal and cosmic. Persons in this stage of development can see themselves as part of the ongoing flow of humanity. They hold the personal and universal together without a sense of opposition and can embrace paradox, inconsistency, and ambiguity with relative ease. They view the vast array of human experience and history from the witness perspective and can respect and value differences while maintaining integrity. Unitives care deeply about the human condition, and from an internalized moral position can respond with justice on behalf of the whole. Without elaborate ego defenses, Unitives are non-attached to outcomes and non-judgmental toward others.

Greater numbers of humans are moving into the Construct-Aware and Unitive stages of development, a movement that can be measured and described. In an evolutionary universe it would seem necessary that the new consciousness be grounded in the material world of human experience. Our dream of a new reality that flows out of a new kind of human, far from being fantasy, is grounded in measurable, tangible experience. These stages of development that are not entirely new but are emerging in greater numbers suggest an increase in morphic resonance in this particular field, and an increase in resonance means that others will be able to enter the morphogenic field of postautonomous ego development with a little more ease. Each person will still be required to do the necessary groundwork to get there, each person will go through the various stages of evolution, but the growing strength of the field itself will be a powerful attractor. The center of gravity, rather than remaining at the Conventional level, will steadily shift upward.

A CONTEMPLATIVE PAUSE

Settle into a quiet inner space, take a few deep relaxing breaths, and then, when you are ready, enter into the following exercises.

- I consider insights within me that have come throughout this chapter. Where is there resonance? Where is there resistance? Where is the realignment?

- What are elements of "postautonomous ego development" that I recognize in myself? Where do I see myself growing in the awareness that I am not separate from all that is? How do I see this awareness influencing my thinking, my speech, my actions?

- What are the challenges that I see as I move to a new worldview? What old beliefs may need to be retired, relegated to a former holon level? What image draws me toward a new worldview?

- I look at my personal journey as one of increasing embrace. What or whom am I able to embrace now that I could not embrace before? What or whom do I struggle to embrace today?

A PRAYER

God of All Creation, you call each of us to evolve, to recognize that you hold all that is in your loving embrace. As we grow in your love, may we learn to hold others in an ever expanding embrace as well. May we see the entire sweep of history as your self-communication that calls us to awaken to who we are in you—and who you are in us. In the mutual embrace that we share, may we together hold the entire cosmos, each and every person, each and every creature, in a way that nurtures and sustains and calls forth the gifts that are given for all. May each of us participate fully in a personal evolution that transforms us and transforms the world. Amen.

Meditation

The soul's center is God. When it has reached God with all the capacity of its being and the strength of its operation and inclination, it will have attained to its final and deepest center in God, it will know, love and enjoy God with all its might.

John of the Cross

Let me seek, then, the gift of silence, and poverty, and solitude, where everything I touch is turned into prayer: where the sky is my prayer, the birds are my prayers, the wind in the trees is my prayer, for God is all in all.

Thomas Merton

In 1982 a team of scientists performed an experiment with three Tibetan Buddhist monks. They placed the monks in a very cold room, attached sensors to their hands and feet, then asked them to meditate. Within minutes all three monks were able to achieve substantial changes in the temperature readings of their fingers and toes. One monk was able to raise his body temperature almost 15° F. Other monks who train in the same tradition have been known to dry ice-cold sheets

that were draped over their bodies as they meditated outside
during frigid Himalayan nights.[1]

Every major religious tradition has meditation practices
that facilitate the entrance into altered states of consciousness. Over time such a discipline affects the abiding state
of consciousness in which the person normally lives. Prayer,
centering, yoga, various forms of meditation—any valid
practice sustained over time will affect the way the person
operates in the world. In recent decades science has begun
to explore not only the results of meditation but the process
itself, notably what happens in the brain when someone
meditates over an extended period of time.

The human brain is divided into left and right hemispheres that are joined by a small bridge of connective tissue
called the corpus callosum. In general, the left hemisphere
governs more analytical functions such as language and
skilled movements, while the right hemisphere governs the
discrimination of shapes, the expression of emotions, the
comprehension of figurative language, as well as holistic pro-
cessing. The left brain is therefore more verbal and processes
in an analytic and linear way, while the right brain is more
visual and processes in a more holistic and intuitive way.

For the vast majority of people, both brain hemispheres
are active and necessary. At the same time, however, each
of us tends to access one hemisphere more than the other,
creating a state of imbalance called lateralization. Bill Harris
of Centerpointe Research Institute says, "Because the brain
filters and interprets reality in a split-brained way, we tend
to see things as separate and opposed, rather than as connected." He adds, "At a deep level, the dual structure of our
brain, in conjunction with brain lateralization, predisposes
us to see and experience ourselves as separate from, and often
in opposition to, the rest of the world."[2]

According to Harris, the greater the lateralization in the brain—that is, the more one hemisphere dominates over the other—the greater will be the experience of separation from the world. As a result, a person experiencing intense lateralization can often feel isolated, fearful, anxious, and stressed (Harris associates addictive behavior with more extreme imbalance). Conversely, the more the hemispheres are in balance (the lesser the degree of lateralization), the greater the sense of the "elegant interconnectedness between us and everything else."[3]

Meditation helps eliminate lateralization, Harris says. The act of focusing on an object, repeating a mantra, attending to the breath, staring at a candle flame, or other similar techniques will begin to synchronize the two hemispheres of the brain. The more concentrated the focus, the deeper will be the meditation, and the deeper the meditation, the more the brain will be synchronized.[4] Done consistently over time, the sense of separation will begin to diminish, replaced by an increased awakening to a connectedness to all that is.

During normal attention or waking consciousness, our brain registers electrical patterns resonating between 13 and 100+ Hz (cycles per second). This beta brain state is associated with attentiveness, arousal, and cognition, with the higher ranges linked to anxiety, uneasiness, distress, and the "flight or fight" response.[5] As a result of meditation, the brain relaxes. The slowing down allows it to enter the alpha brain wave state, which resonates between 8 and 12.9 Hz. The alpha state is associated with relaxation, pre-sleep or pre-awakening, drowsiness, and introspection. The deeper or lower end of the alpha range is the pattern most associated with meditation and is characterized by contentment and peace. While very experienced meditators can reach the theta stage (4–7.9 Hz), these experiences are usually not sustained over long periods of time. The theta state is associated with rapid eye movement (REM) sleep, increased creativity, healing, memory, and integrative experiences. The slowest brain wave state is the delta state, the pattern of dreamless sleep that runs at 0.1–3.9 Hz. Amazingly, it is in fact possible to remain awake during delta if small amounts of beta, alpha, and theta are also present. We normally have more than one wave state running simultaneously, but one pattern or another will dominate consciousness.[6]

As meditation practice continues, there is a change in the brain itself. "As the meditator accesses these more relaxed meditative brain wave states, there is an increase in communication (and therefore balance) between the two sides of the brain, and a reduction in feelings of stress and separation."[7] Harris explains that over time the practice of meditation results in the formation of neural connections between the two hemispheres. In effect, we are "rewired." This rewiring will eventually lead to "an ability to enter these altered states at will, even when not meditating, and remain in them for longer and longer periods."[8] Remaining in these states for longer and longer periods eventually changes our perspective, a characteristic of the move from one developmental stage to the next.

We have already looked at Susanne Cook-Greuter's work, which found that as we progress through the stages of psychological development, we undergo shifts in our worldview. These shifts amount to both a growing sense of wholeness and a more inclusive embrace of the world. As we grow, an ever deepening sense of connectedness grows as well, until finally, we reach a state of cosmic consciousness in which we live out of the perception that all life is fundamentally a single reality, a state of nonduality. Having more and more human beings come to this stage of development could have a tremendous impact on the world in which we live. With greater numbers of people living out of the awareness that all life is connected, it would only be a matter of time before systems and institutions would evolve toward greater inclusion and a larger embrace. What Harris's research suggests is that meditation can be a vehicle that takes us to these higher stages of human development.

What part, if any, can organized religion play in facilitating these higher stages of development? One of Ken Wilber's critiques of religious traditions is that while they have done well in acknowledging altered states of consciousness, they have, for the most part, failed to make a connection between the *states* of consciousness that occur during prayer and meditation and *stages* of consciousness that are the result of developmental growth. Religious traditions know about the power of prayer and meditation. What they tend to speak less about is how this power results in real human growth and development—both individual and communal. Someone in the Conventional stage of development may experience deep alpha waves in meditation, may have an experience of deep connectedness to the whole, but will nevertheless remain Conventional in the interpretation of the experience until the shift to the next stage of consciousness occurs. Deep alpha for the postautonomous adult will manifest in a greater sense of connectedness than for the Conventional adult. The *stage* of consciousness or development is as significant as the *state* of consciousness. Research suggests that the more the deeper states of consciousness are sustained, the more likely the person will evolve to the next higher stage of development. This happens through the practice of meditation. Wilber says:

> . . . considerable research has demonstrated that the
> more you experience meditative or contemplative states

of consciousness, the faster you develop through the stages of consciousness. No other single practice or technique—not therapy, not breath work, not transformative workshops, not role-taking, not *hatha yoga*—has been empirically demonstrated to do this. Meditation alone has done so.[9]

However, it is important to recognize that even as the person moves more quickly through the stages, none of them can be skipped. We must go through stage one, then two, then three. Meditation does not allow the person to skip any stage; it simply facilitates the movement so that transition from stage to stage happens a little more rapidly.

At each stage of development there is a certain characteristic sense of self (or phase of ego development) that a person holds. Each person is embedded in this sense of self, the subjective ground out of which she or he functions. Each self-sense is like a particular lens through which the individual views reality. It determines just about everything: worldview, beliefs, perceptions, how data is interpreted, behavior, emotional responses, moral character, motivation, defense mechanisms, decision making, language, interaction with others and the world. This sense of self is an entire bundle of root beliefs, perceptions, and interactions that determine how the person functions. With sustained meditation, however, the straps that hold the bundle together begin to loosen. Incongruities filter into awareness, and old perceptions begin to untether. As the person begins the shift to the new stage of consciousness, she or he begins to witness what is emerging—to notice what is happening within. This may come quite subtly, but the result is that what used to be a subjective sense of self now becomes objective. The person is no longer embedded in this particular sense of self, which now becomes the object of a new subjective sense of self that is emerging. Thus the subject of one stage becomes the object of the next, over and over again as we make our way through stage after stage. The role of meditation in the process—the reason it facilitates a quicker move through the stages—is that it is essentially a practice in witnessing. It teaches the meditator to make the subject an object while learning to observe interior movements that occur during meditation.

What Is Meditation?

Up until this point, I have been using the term "meditation" in a rather broad sense, indicating any practice that requires the sustained attention necessary to enable a person to enter an altered state of consciousness while remaining fully awake and alert. In this sense, meditation is not definitively connected with any particular religion or denomination but can be used by any person as a tool for consciously engaging the transcendent dimension of human experience. This may seem a somewhat vague description—it is purposefully so. Sometimes our very own religious doctrines and beliefs, our own images of ourselves and of God, can hinder our experience of the Holy. I grew up with the belief that God was literally a man sitting on a throne in some other spatial dimension called Heaven, and this supported an image of God as male, distant, and in demand of perfection. I know many adults who still have this kind of image of God. We all have, at the very least, remnants of images of God that are simply illusory. We often confuse God with Santa Claus and think that if our performance is up to specifications (our own, certainly not God's), life will be reward-filled and suffering-free. As long as we cling to childish images of God, we cannot become spiritually mature. Therefore, an essential component of meditation becomes the willingness to leave everything—*everything*—behind, including our most cherished images of God. Whatever we think or imagine, no matter how true it may be, is not God, the incomprehensible holy mystery beyond any thought or image.

A few years ago I saw a short video entitled *Movie 15* produced by Daniel J. Simons of the Visual Cognition Lab at the University of Illinois. In this video, there are two teams of three persons each, one team wearing white shirts and the other team black. Each team is engaged in passing a basketball among themselves. As the passing begins, the viewer is given instructions to count the number of times the basketballs are passed. While the balls are being passed, right in the middle of the film (the film lasts only about thirty seconds), a person dressed in a gorilla costume walks through the middle of all the basketballs being passed, stops, beats its chest, then walks off.

When the video is complete, the viewer is asked how many times the basketball was passed. The viewer is also asked, "Did you see anything unusual?" Results from the lab indicated that over half of the time viewers took no notice of the gorilla. This strange phenomenon is known as "inattentional blindness." Simons writes, "Objects can pass through the spatial extent of attentional focus . . . and still not be 'seen' if they are not specifically being attended."[10] So often we see only what we intend to see, what we believe to be there. Having our attention already filled with what we think we know and believe to be true can render us blind to what is really there. When we go into meditation clinging to what we think we know, we set ourselves up for inattentional blindness, unaware of the new that is seeking to emerge.

Meditation, then, is not about holding any particular belief or doctrine but has to do with allowing us to live in a space that exposes our illusions and false notions of the holy and of life itself. Meditation is also about learning to live in the present moment, to live fully in the now rather than in the past or the future. Meditation teaches us how to be present, first to ourselves and to God, and then to the whole world. Meditation is about allowing our dysfunctions and addictions to reveal themselves, not so that we can judge them, but so they can be released of their power to drain life from us. Meditation is about becoming a witness, not attached to any particular sense of self, but simply learning to mindfully observe that which arises and passes.

No matter what our religious convictions, meditation will help clarify our own personal truths in a way that resonates with our tradition. Meditation enables a Christian to become a better Christian, a Buddhist to become a better Buddhist, a Hindu to become a better Hindu, and so on. Ultimately it takes the Christian beyond Christianity, the Buddhist beyond Buddhism, the Hindu beyond Hinduism—it must, because the incomprehensible holy mystery that is part of the experience of every human, whatever or however we may name it, is beyond the power of any single institution or system to hold. Incomprehensible also means uncontrollable, and the mystics of every tradition tell us that this is so.

The purpose of meditation is not about being in control. It is about being in the heart and hands of the uncontrollable. It must therefore be free of agenda and attachment to ideas, ideologies, institutions, dysfunctions, addictions, or fears. Although tradition helps us enter, even tradition must be abandoned in the moment of meditation so that we may be unfettered and free to receive what mystery may have to offer.

How possible is this kind of letting go? It is entirely possible, yet it may take years of practice and personal evolution to get there. As with any significant endeavor, we aim the highest that we can and go from there, aware that what we are aiming for is an ever-receding horizon, not a well-defined final destination. We must know that the letting go will go in cycles, that there will be times that we feel we have arrived, followed by times that we wonder what happened to our well-formed intention. There will be times when meditation is effortless and times when it becomes a dreaded chore. But at some point we will come to know that meditation sustains us, moves us, sets us free for self-transcendence, and enables us to hold the entire world that so needs our embrace.

At some point in our practice of meditation (as in life itself) we will move past the need to "let go" and instead be open to the desire to "let come." If it is true that our lives unfold in the direction of the vision that we hold, then the movement to a stance of "let come" is essential. What I long ago noticed in myself was that when I am focused on letting go, I am usually focused on what I don't want. If I am focused on not judging, the focus is still on judging—much like when I try not to think of a purple teddy bear, I think of a purple teddy bear. For me the image of letting go presupposes attachment, a holding on to something that is keeping me from freely turning to receive that which is emerging. If, on the other hand, I am guided by "let come," I find myself in the witness stance, attentive and open to what is emerging, and therefore more able to participate in that which incomprehensible holy mystery is communicating.

The Components of Meditation

For those who do not have a meditation practice, there are many resources for learning. The work of Thomas Keating teaches the practice known as centering prayer, while James Finley teaches Christian meditation. Pema Chödrön and Jack Kornfield are teachers in the Buddhist tradition. Spiritual directors normally can facilitate meditation practice, as can yoga instructors. What is significant is to find a practice that suits you, one that fits your temperament and style. For some people, a repetitive practice like the rosary leads into meditation; for others, slow, intentional walking induces a deeper state of consciousness. For many, the repetition of a mantra or the counting of breaths is what works. What is important is that you find one practice and remain faithful to it over time. While experimenting with new techniques can be helpful, especially if you have not yet identified one that you want to make your own, it is not helpful to skip around from practice to practice. Commit to one practice or path, and let that one guide you.

Most meditation practices have common elements that help facilitate the habit, especially sitting meditation, which is what I will focus on here. First, meditation must have the proper setting. A quiet place free from distraction of any kind is important. Turn off the electronics and create an ambiance that is conducive to silence. Decide what length of time you are able to devote to sitting. If you are a beginner, or if time is pressing, choose five or ten minutes. If you are more experienced and have more time, choose from twenty minutes to an hour. What is important in regard to time is to do what is possible. I remember as a young mother feeling a bit guilty that I could never seem to get more than ten or fifteen minutes of quiet time in which to meditate. It is not helpful to enter into meditation with guilt or any other feeling that will get in the way. Your time is what it is; simply commit to what is possible, even if only two minutes, and that will be fine.

The next thing to consider is posture. While I sometimes like to use a meditation pillow, most of the time I sit in a chair in which my feet can rest flat on the floor. Posture is important because it is related to breathing and grounding, getting connected to yourself and Earth while opening to the transcendent. As you sit with feet flat on the floor, imagine that an energetic pole is running through your spine, extending downward into Earth, extending upward to the heavens. Gently move your focus to your hips and buttocks, and allow yourself to relax and sink deeply into the chair. Sit for a moment in that awareness, then take your focus to the soles of your feet. Imagine that the Earth energy coming from three thousand feet down is passing slowly yet potently through your feet, up through your legs, into your torso, then into your heart. Attend to the energy, imagine that it is happening, know that it is happening whether you "feel" it or not.

After a few moments—and there is no reason to rush any of this process—imagine that the energy, which you may want to image as divine light, is entering your body through the top of your head, filling your brain, relaxing your face, your ears, your shoulders, your neck, your arms, until finally the light rests in your heart. Notice that in your heart the energy of Earth and the energy of the incomprehensible holy mystery have converged. Sit with that awareness for a few moments. Do not make an effort to relax; rather, allow relaxation to come over you.

If this movement quiets you and brings you to a place beyond thought, stay with it. That is where you want to go. If, however, thoughts begin to come, you may choose to use a mantra (a sacred word or phrase) or attend to the breath. The meaning of the word is not as significant as the use of the word. Its repetition will help facilitate your moving into a deeper meditative space.

Another option is to attend to the breath, which can simply be the noticing of inhalation and exhalation or the counting of the breaths, starting over each time you fall into distraction. The significance of focusing on a word or the breath is that it takes you beyond words. It is the rhythmic repetition and its ability to focus attention that moves you into a place where thoughts and the words that hold them can evaporate. Repetition is important in two ways. First, the repetition of a mantra or the focus on the breath in a meditation session helps one move into that sacred space beyond words and thoughts. Second, repetition over time—staying faithful to the practice day after day, year after year—will help sustain each new level of consciousness that emerges.

Buddhists have a phrase that refers to the incessant chatter that we all experience during times of meditation. "Monkey mind" refers to the sometimes endless mental prattle that goes on in our heads, and frequently our meditation sessions are overcome by its noise. This is perhaps the location of greatest disappointment and frustration for beginning meditators. At times the entire session seems to be filled with this chatter, and it can seem that nothing of significance is happening. But that is not the case. Something is always happening when you sit with intention. The moment you try to stop yourself from thinking, you are thinking, so the only helpful way to respond is to return to the word or the breath without judgment. Simply notice the thoughts, then return to your practice.

It is important not to judge your meditation—whether a particular practice session or the way you think it is going over time. Observe it, witness it, notice how things are going, invite the help of those with experience—but do not judge. Use your observations to reflect on your own capacities as a holon, make efforts to evolve, but do not judge. So what if you ended your session early? So what if you found yourself making a to-do list? It is not the end of the world, and you are not a substandard meditator. Simply begin again. That's all. Start all over. No moment of intention and striving is lost, but judgment engages the ego and is not helpful at all. Do not judge.

For those who meditate over time, the experience continues to deepen. It is difficult to speak of what happens, and it seems that each practitioner describes the experience in a different way. Some say it is like coming into a great light or a place of peace, while others describe the experience as darkness or being in a great abyss or "no-thing." Whatever words are used, there tends to be an experience of nonduality, of being inseparable from the ground of all being, of being unable to distinguish between consciousness of the self and mystery. And while words and images can help facilitate our getting there, in this deep meditative place there are no words, no thoughts, no images. There is just reality itself, incomprehensible holy mystery, totally accessible yet completely ineffable. It goes away as subtly as it comes, yet something of its essence lingers, just beyond the senses. That is the "taste" of meditation that comes unannounced. It is profoundly powerful.

When the meditation period ends, come out gently. Close with a prayer or affirmation, reorient yourself, then get up slowly. Before you close, you may want to ask what your intention is for the day. How will you manifest the love and peace you have experienced? How will you make incomprehensible holy mystery tangible in your own life and the life of others today? As we continue to meditate over time, we notice that less and less is left behind when we move into our day. Peace abides. Comfort with oneself remains. Love permeates thoughts and actions, and we are solidly grounded in the present moment. This is why we meditate. It helps us become who we are.

A commitment to meditation may not lead us to become like the Tibetan monks who can raise their body temperatures through meditation, but it can raise consciousness— our own consciousness, and through us, the consciousness of the world. Meditation, while a component of every major religious tradition, is not about religious belief. It is about transformation. Meditation enables us to move to the place of witness, and from there become the unattached observer, the one who can let come that which incomprehensible holy mystery seeks to give.

On the physiological level, meditation diminishes the lateralization of the left and right hemispheres of the brain, reducing the feeling of separation and augmenting a greater sense of harmony with the world. As a result, we grow in our sense of connectedness and embrace. While meditation can bring us to altered states of consciousness, its value lies in its ability to facilitate our movement through the stages of adult growth and development so that we may participate in the transformation of consciousness that is essential in our moment of time.

Meditation helps loosen the grip of the sense of self that experiences separation and disconnection and facilitates a shift to the place of witness where the subjective self is observed. This observation lessens identification with that sense of self, enabling the person's perspective to expand. The subject becomes the object, and self-transcendence ensues.

Meditation is not a way to control reality. Rather, it is a practice that allows us to place ourselves in the hands of the uncontrollable. Meditation helps release our grip on everything, including religious beliefs and images of God, constructs that attempt to put words on what is ineffable.

As helpful as beliefs and images have been, there comes a point at which we let go of even these things—and free fall into incomprehensible holy mystery. As we allow our grasp of images and our desire for particular experiences to loosen, we are set free from the inattentional blindness that keeps us from seeing clearly. We become more open to the incomprehensible holy mystery at the heart of what is real.

While there are many practices that are helpful, what is essential is to be grounded in one practice that is holistic—that engages the whole body and allows the mind to cease its endless chatter, eventually leading to ever deeper experiences of the ground of all being. In that place of nonduality, in that place of unity in which we cease to know ourselves as separate from all that is holy, we are transformed, and as we exit that holy of holies and re-enter the external world, we become instruments of co-creativity who invite others into transformation as well.

A CONTEMPLATIVE PAUSE

Settle into a quiet inner space, take a few deep relaxing breaths, and then, when you are ready, enter into the following exercises.

- I consider insights within me that have come throughout this chapter. Where is there resonance? Where is there resistance? Where is the realignment?

- Where have I experienced inattentional blindness, and how does that affect both myself and others?

- If I do not meditate, I consider it as a practice. If I already have a meditation practice, I witness it, simply observing it as it is without judgment. What do I see?

A PRAYER

Incomprehensible Holy Mystery, so often I am blind to your self-communication. So often I fail to see your love that is in plain view. Help me to see. Release me from my inattentional blindness, and allow me to truly see what is before me. May I release myself and others from judgment, and may I discover in the silence who I am in you and who you are in me. Enable me to grow into a maturity that embraces the world and participates co-creatively in the life of the world. May all creation benefit from my practice of meditation. Amen.

chapter
eight

The Power of
Intention

*By transforming our consciousness, we participate in the
transformation of the world.*

Robert Thurman

What if a thought can heal the world?

Lynne McTaggart

In the first three months of 1998, forest fires raged in the
northern Brazilian state of Roraima, devastating more than
20 percent of the cultivated land. There had been no rainfall
for six months, a condition thought to be caused by El Niño.
The forecast was bleak: no rain was predicted until April.
The blaze destroyed more than one and a half million acres
of highland savannah, and another twelve million acres—an
area larger than The Netherlands—were threatened. Nearly
thirty thousand people—farmers and their families whose
lives depended on the land—were affected by the fire, and
many of them had no water or food. One of the hardest hit
communities was the Yanomami Indian Reservation. Despite

the efforts of fourteen hundred firefighters that included volunteers from Argentina and Venezuela, the three-month inferno could not be brought under control. "It is an impossible mission," said one member of the multinational firefighting team. Only heavy rain—not yet in the forecast—could douse the flames.

With fires advancing into the rain forest, something had to be done. "The fires are taking over our land, killing the animals we hunt and the birds in the trees," said Yanomami leader Davi Kopenawa. "We need help because the rains are still a long way off." On March 29 help came. Two shamans from the Kaiapo tribe were called inside the Yanomami reservation and asked to intervene. "They are going to hold a ceremony," said one government official. "It is a ritual to repel smoke and, if possible, bring on rain." According to reports, the shamans performed their ancient ritual on the banks of a dried-up river. Hours later, rain fell so hard that airplanes that had been dropping water on the fires could not take off.[1]

What happened in Roraima? Is it possible that the energy of the shamans brought on the rain that wasn't supposed to come for several weeks? Did the two of them cause the rain or influence the rain? Did the rain come as a result of the supplication of many who were affected by the fire or by others outside the community who extended care and concern? The story is not at all uncommon. Many of us have experiences in which our thoughts or prayers seemed to have an impact on the outcome of a situation, and often we intuitively sense the truth of those experiences, even when we cannot explain them.

We know from quantum physics that everything is connected. The principle known as nonlocality or quantum entanglement says that once two particles have connected, they remain connected, no matter what the spatial distance. A few centimeters or across the universe, the connection remains. It was once thought that the phenomenon of non-locality pertained only to the subatomic realm, but recent experiments have demonstrated that this is not the case, that atoms—considered "big" on the quantum scale—also participate in quantum entanglement.[2]

Quantum physics says that a subatomic particle remains in a state of probability or "superposition" until an observer gets involved. The observer helps bring about that which is observed. Current research has shown that the observer effect is not restricted to the quantum realm, but manifests in the "ordinary" world as well. Lynne McTaggart states that it appears "that the most essential ingredient in creating our universe is the consciousness that observes it." She notes: "Reality is not fixed, but fluid, or mutable, and hence possibly open to influence."[3] Does this explain why it rained soon after the shamans performed their ritual? Does this suggest that we may have influence over events in our own lives? Perhaps it is so. "Cocreation and influence," McTaggart says, "may be a basic, inherent property of life."

In her book *The Intention Experiment*, McTaggart examines recent research that looks at the implications of quantum physics, particularly in the ways we may potentially influence the world around us. Using studies that follow the strictest scientific protocol, McTaggart considers the evidence that suggests we have the capacity to affect what happens in our lives though intentionality. She defines an intention as "a purposeful plan to perform an action, which will lead to a desired outcome."[4] While it is a long jump from quantum physics and controlled laboratory experiments to the assertion that we influence what becomes manifest, research suggests that this may very well be the case.

As each of us moves, we generate an electrical charge. "Every movement we make appears to be felt by the people around us," McTaggart says.[5] If our energy does in fact touch others, each movement creates a relationship. Citing work by Stanford physicist William Tiller, she says that "directed thoughts produce demonstrable physical energy, even over remote distance."[6] Thoughts intended for healing are subject to measurement as well. Bernard Grad, from McGill University in Montreal, examined the effect of sending healing energy into water, discovering that water treated by healers had undergone a fundamental change in its molecular structure.[7] McTaggart concludes that the kinds of changes affected by healing energy can occur through the act of intention.

Other studies also suggest that our energy does indeed affect others. In the 1970s German physicist Fritz-Albert Popp demonstrated that all living things, from simple, unicellular organisms to complex human beings, radiate a steady stream of photons—that is, light. He called this stream of light "biophoton emission" and postulated that this kind of radiation is the perfect medium for transferring information within the organism. It is entirely possible that molecules communicate with other molecules in a body through light waves that act like a tuning fork, allowing molecules to behave in concert with one another, giving the body coherence.

Popp also discovered that light is somehow communicated *between* organisms. Carrying the work further, Gary Schwartz, a psychophysiologist from the University of Arizona, verified that biophoton emission can pass from organism to organism. In an experiment with Kathy Creath, a professor of optical sciences at Arizona, the two researchers used a specialized camera to photograph light being emitted from a geranium leaf. For the first time it was possible to see light emanating from a living thing, findings that have been confirmed by other researchers. Next, they photographed the hands of people known as healers. Remarkably, they captured images of waves of light as it flowed from their fingers. Schwartz concluded that the intention of healing creates waves of light that pass from healer to subject.[8] What McTaggart adds is that "every last thought appeared to augment or diminish something else's light."[9]

Studies show that setting an intention and sending healing energy has a physical effect on the recipient. "When you send an intention, every major physiological system in your body is mirrored in the body of the receiver."[10] In addition, when the energy of two people comes together, the one with "the most cohesive quantum waves" will often set the tempo for the other. "The most ordered brain pattern often prevailed."[11] In other words, when a peaceful person sends calming thoughts, the recipient registers the peace in his or her body in a way that is measurable.

In 1665, a Dutch mathematician by the name of Christiaan Huygens discovered that when two or more clocks were in close proximity, they would eventually begin to swing in unison. This phenomenon is known as entrainment. Physicists say that entrainment occurs as tiny bits of energy are exchanged when two systems are out of sync. The exchange of energy causes one system to slow down and the other to accelerate so that they come into phase, a phenomenon closely related to resonance. Everything that vibrates has its own preferred frequencies, called "resonant frequencies." McTaggart says that when a system "listens" or receives a vibration from another, "it tunes out all pretenders and only tunes into its own resonant frequency."[12] Once systems have entrained and "march to the same rhythm," they send out a stronger signal together than they did separately.[13]

In another study Dr. Rollin McCraty, who directs the research for the Institute of HeartMath in Boulder Creek, California, explored feelings of foreboding of an event and the physical effect of such events. What McCraty discovered was that the presentiment of either good or bad news was registered both in the heart and the brain. Electromagnetic waves would either speed up or slow down before a disturbing or tranquil picture was shown. Interestingly, the heart seemed to pick up the information *before* the brain. McTaggart says that this suggests that "the body has certain perceptual apparatus that enables it continually to scan and intuit the future, but that the heart may hold the largest antenna."[14] McCraty found that entrainment that registered in the brain occurred when people touched or even focused on the heart.[15]

Another fascinating study is being conducted under the direction of Roger Nelson, the former director of the Princeton Engineering Anomalies Research. The Global Consciousness Project, which began in 1998, explores the possibility of group consciousness. The study uses sixty-five Random Event Generators (also called REGs or EGGs), which are electronic devices set up all over the world to generate random numbers—much like the toss of a coin. The project is designed to see if significant world events impact the randomness of the REGs. The first event that registered occurred soon after the project began in August 1998—the bombings of the U.S. embassies in Nairobi and Tanzania. Other events included the tragic train crash in India and the One Billion Person Meditation in 1999, the Global Group Mind Meditation in 2000, the terrorist attacks in the United States and Ramadan meditation in 2001, the terrorist attacks in Madrid and the deaths of Russian school hostages in 2004, the Indonesian earthquake in 2006, and the nomination and election of Barack Obama in 2008. The evidence points toward the existence of a collective consciousness that can be measured and possibly predict that significant events are about to occur.[16]

According to McTaggart, the work of the Global Consciousness Project offers clues about the nature of intentions that are held within a group. She writes, "The energy from a collective, intensely felt thought appears to be infectious. There appears to be a 'dose' effect; the effect on REG of a load of people thinking the same thought is larger than the effect of a single person."[17] It seems that the size of the group does not matter as much as the intensity of focus. McTaggart says that "any group, however small, exerted an effect so long as the parties were involved in rapturous attention."[18]

While viewing her work as far from complete, McTaggart comes to some pretty strong conclusions:

> We can no longer view ourselves as isolated from our environment, and our thoughts as the private, self-contained workings of an individual brain. . . . As observers and creators, we are constantly remaking our world at every instant. Every thought we have, every judgment we hold, however unconscious, is having an effect. With every moment that it notices, the conscious mind is sending an intention.[19]

In light of the research, stories like that of the shamans and forest fire in Roraima do not seem so far-fetched after all. Experiments now demonstrate that the observer effect is quite real, and not only on the subatomic level. We do influence our world by the intentions we create, either consciously or unconsciously. Every movement we make, every thought we generate, impacts reality in some measurable way. Our energy is intertwined with all the energy that is. That is the simple truth.

In working with groups I often use an educational tool called the Energy Ball to demonstrate just how connected we are. About the size and weight of a ping pong ball, the device is equipped with two small electrodes. If you touch the electrodes simultaneously, creating a closed circuit, the ball flashes with light and emits a warbling sound. I have used the Energy Ball with groups as large as a hundred, and when we all hold hands and two of us then complete the circuit by touching the electrodes, the ball lights up and makes the warbling sound. When any two people break their handhold, thus breaking the connection of the whole group, the light and sound cease but resume once the hands are joined again. It is an amazing demonstration of the electron flow that connects us.[20]

Each of us, as we move, affects the energy around us. Each of us emits a particular quality of light or radiance called biophoton emission. Each of us resonates with the frequencies with which we most identify. And once we get a certain kind of energy going, the entrainment or resonance of that energy strengthens. If our resonance is negative, our energy moves in that direction; if our resonance is positive, our energy moves in that direction.

It seems that not only our brain or our eyes are receptors, but every part of our body is involved in the energetic dance. Our heart knows just as much as our head, perhaps even more. It seems plausible that what we consider to be "mind" is not merely a function of the brain but a whole-body experience. Research also suggests that much of our consciousness operates in a subtle way. On an unconscious yet collective level, we are connected to all that is happening on the planet. We are constantly influencing and being influenced, entraining and resonating, emitting positive or negative energy, affecting and being affected by all that is. Although we may think that we function as separate persons, at every second we are caught in a web of interconnected and interdependent relationships that shape what we call reality.

What do these findings mean in terms of morphogenic fields? The results of an abundance of research suggest that the hypothesis of morphogenic fields is entirely plausible. Experiments can demonstrate that non-material regions of influence around a holon or system do indeed exist and can be measured. The strength of these fields magnifies as the resonance increases, whether that resonance is augmented individually or collectively. If, as these studies suggest, we are constantly influencing and even creating new fields all the time, then would it not be prudent to be intentional about maintaining those that are life-giving? This is not to suggest mere wishful thinking, of pinning our hopes on fantasy, but engaging all the co-creative power we have to make choices that will save rather than imperil the whole. It will be a most difficult task. It will require the full use of all our capacities as holons, all the freedom we possess, all the compassion that can flow from us. The sacrifice it calls for will be the paschal mystery of our time as it entails the willingness to go to our deaths for the sake of the life of the whole. Yes, it is a difficult task, and yet it may well be the only viable option that remains.

A CONTEMPLATIVE PAUSE

Settle into a quiet inner space, take a few deep relaxing breaths, and then, when you are ready, enter into the following exercises.

- I consider insights within me that have come throughout this chapter. Where is there resonance? Where is there resistance? Where is the realignment?

- I recall the times I have been intentional about a situation and feel that I affected the outcome. I observe times that I have been intentional but the event did not unfold as I wanted. What insights surface?

- I consider groups to which I belong that imply intentionality. How might we become more intentional?

A PRAYER

Holy One, we believe that each of us lives because of your divine intention. You set your mind on us 13.7 billion years ago, and we have been moving toward your vision for eons. As we strive to respond to your self-communication to us, as we resolve to be open to your grace, help us to be intentional about who we are and who we are to become. May we use the gift of intentionality wisely, knowing that the resonance of our spirits impacts each and every one we meet. May we resonate with love, helping to build a field of compassion that transforms the world. Amen.

chapter nine

The Fields Converge

When you act on behalf
of something greater than yourself,
you begin
to feel it acting through you
with a power that is greater than your own.

Joanna Macy

The universe is a unity—an interacting, evolving, and genetically-related community of being bound together inseparably in space and time. Our responsibilities to each other and to all of creation are implicit on this unity. Each of us is profoundly implicated in the functioning and fate of every other being on the planet, and ultimately, perhaps, throughout the universe.

Chet Raymo

This book began with an invitation to take up the challenge of our time—and the story of the rescue of the whales set the stage for our discussion. In this particular moment in time, we are faced with crises that threaten to overwhelm us with both their enormity as well as their sheer quantity.

The whales that confront us are so big, and we are so small. It is easy to slide into fear-filled paralysis, especially when we see no clear way through or have nothing tangible to offer in response. It is understandable that when faced with the immensity of the challenge we want to turn and run, for it is difficult to know where to begin. *Field of Compassion* seeks to find a way to respond so that we may face our challenges straight on and with the very best that we have to offer.

We know that turnaround is required. Only a different course than the one that prevails in our culture will save us—and we are the ones who must facilitate the turning. Our salvation will not involve an extraordinary rescue by an extraordinary deity. It will not come from exceptional superheroes. The rescue will come from ordinary human beings like you and me. It is as simple as that. We may imagine that we are ill-equipped for such a daunting task, but I hope that as you have read these chapters, you will have grown in the recognition that we have been prepared.

In this chapter I would like to bring together the pieces that we have engaged thus far—to point out ways in which they connect and form a whole, suggesting we are ready for the challenge. We have been gifted with capacities that empower us to be agents of transformation. We have been given stories to move us and images to engage us. We have been granted a unique glimpse of the cosmos that brings us to awe and wonder. We have seen the tiniest forms of life and been shown that we ourselves are participants in an energetic dance of life. We have all that we need; we must now become all that we can be.

The Significance of Our Stories

We understand and live our lives in and through stories, the bones upon which we hang the flesh of our lives. We have acknowledged, as Thomas Berry has pointed out, that our generation is one that is between stories—between the scientific and religious, between the old and the new. But the other side—the place where all stories can meet and dialogue and discover their common truths—is in sight.

We have also acknowledged the power of an image. Our mind takes what we focus upon as the invitation to make it happen. We are drawn toward images that empower us with their energy. This is why we must take great care in sorting out the images we carry, discarding those that no longer serve to connect us to our capacities and power, embracing those that empower us to live with greater integrity.

The Universe Story has been a catalyst for our generation's movement toward a deeper, fuller, richer narrative that holds our experience of life itself in a coherent way. For 13.7 billion years our universe has been evolving, moving in the direction of increasing complexity and greater consciousness. The cosmos itself is predominantly invisible, held together and expanded by the forces known as dark matter and dark energy. The Universe Story moves us into a place where we may witness the big picture, where we can stand back and glimpse the evolutionary process of which we have been a part. Being in this space is no less significant than our witness of Earth from space for the first time in 1968. This view of cosmic history pulls us toward cosmic consciousness.

The Universe Story also moves us into the space where we see the tiny picture—where we grasp the minute details that suggest how intricately woven creation is. The Universe Story from the quantum or subatomic realm demonstrates that life is primarily an energetic dance, and that we are all partners who sway in rhythm and create the dance each and every moment of our lives. Quantum physics gives us a glimpse of how potent our energy is. The principle of non-locality suggests that once we have touched, we are forever partners in some unseen and mysterious way. We know that a movement as slight as the ruffle of a butterfly's wing changes energy patterns—alters the dance. And we have learned that somehow the simple act of observation is an integral part of manifestation.

An older story, but one that still has great potency in our culture, is the Christian story. This narrative, too, is an evolutionary one. Christian theology dialogues with other disciplines and is attentive to questions that emerge when circumstances and knowledge change. An old definition of theology is "faith seeking understanding." Theological reflection, at its heart, is about attending to the sacred dimension of our reality, paying attention to the transcendent elements, not in order to proscribe or restrict, but to facilitate both our experience and our reflection upon that experience. It is fair to say that often our interpretations have made it seem as if the holy relates only to those who give assent to particular beliefs, but this certainly is not the case. Surely the One we call God is far beyond our best impulses and not restricted by our worst.

We have examined the work of Karl Rahner as an example of the fullness and richness of the Christian tradition as it dialogues with the Universe Story, particularly the understanding of the evolutionary process itself. Rahner begins with human experience and the hallmarks of what it means to be human. We have the capacity for self-reflective consciousness. We know that we know, we are aware of our subjective self, and our self-awareness is part of every interaction we have. It is part and parcel of the human experience to ask questions, to seek to know, and when we have an answer to one question, that response becomes the ground from which we ask the next question and the one after that. We are seekers of knowledge and truth, always moving toward a horizon that forever recedes.

We also have the capacity for love. Throughout our lives we open ourselves to relationships in which we find communion. We choose to allow others to enter our hearts, and we willingly pour out our care and concern for others in self-sacrificing ways. Like the quest to know, the capacity for love has no limit, for as we grow, so does our embrace of the world around us.

As humans we have the capacity for freedom. The Apostle Paul tells us that it is for freedom that Christ set us free. Freedom was at the center of Jesus' life and ministry. He was continually calling listeners to break through customary restraints and see things differently so that they could choose to live differently. The desire to be free has nothing to do with an egocentric craving to live without restraint. Rather, at its heart, the capacity for freedom underpins our quest for truth and for love. The ways in which we demonstrate our desire for truth and love, when not grounded in genuine freedom, tend to lapse into neurosis and dysfunction.

Our ability to ask questions and seek truth, as well as our capacity for love and freedom, are the result of eons of evolution. Moment by moment, over 13.7 billion years, we inched our way toward this place. Over most of our history we have passively evolved, but in the present age we have come to recognize that these capacities can no longer sit idle or be frivolously occupied. They are gifts intended for engagement. They carry within them an implicit invitation to be co-creators.

Rahner's theology has allowed us to take a cosmic view of Christian religious experience. We live in a world of grace—God's self-communication, the pouring out of God's very self in and for the life of the world. We are surrounded, shaped, and constituted by the grace of a God who is incomprehensible holy mystery, a God who cannot be understood fully, a God whose presence and power are as ineffable as they are real.

God's bestowal of grace began with time itself. It is interwoven in our history. Through the work of the Holy Spirit, all creation has been pressured from within to evolve. Inert matter evolved, becoming ever more conscious, until, at a particular moment in the concrete history of the world, self-reflective consciousness emerged in a species we call human. The material universe that came into existence and was maintained by grace finally became aware of the grace that had been there all along, the self-communication of the Holy that was at the heart of all life.

In the Christian story we locate this moment of evolutionary history in the person of Jesus, the Christ, but we celebrate it in ourselves as well. Jesus was an evolutionary first, a cosmic event that ushered in a new era of profound awareness of how intricately the Holy is woven into the fabric of our lives. Even as we name Jesus the Incarnation, we come to recognize that the Incarnation is not only about a significant human being who lived in first-century Palestine, it is about a significant moment in history for humankind and for all creation.

More than anything else, Jesus signaled a new consciousness—a new way of looking at God, self, and all others. This new consciousness crystallized in the image of the "kingdom of God," the here-and-now reality that he never tired of living and inviting others to enter. The word "incarnation" literally means "in the flesh," and the kingdom of God was the reality in which the consciousness heralded by Jesus could be enfleshed. While the kingdom belonged to God, it was clear that Jesus wanted us to take possession, to occupy its domain. Entrance was free—that is, it would engage our capacity for freedom, it would require that we think and behave and relate to others in self-sacrificing ways that involved the conscious choice to love.

Neil Douglas-Klotz points out that the word Jesus would have used for God is "Alaha," which can be translated as "Sacred Unity, Oneness, the All, the Ultimate Power/ Potential, the One with no opposite." The kingdom of God is primarily a commUnity, a lived experience grounded in relationship with Ultimate Power/Potential, the One with no opposite. It is characterized by freedom and love and the endless quest to know the One and to respond in faithful, tangible ways. Douglas-Klotz also tells us that the Aramaic word usually translated as "kingdom" is *malkuta*, which refers to rule sanctioned by knowledge of the group or the whole of which the one who leads is a part. Those designated to speak for the community were those empowered to say, "Yes, I can," signifying both an understanding of the will of the whole and the ability to enact that will. The kingdom is not about passively occupying a designated place, but about a dynamic life of freedom that understands and moves with the whole. It is a kingdom of Unity—union with incomprehensible holy mystery and union with those whom mystery has created.

The Universe Story, the Christian story, and the story of the kingdom of God are powerful narratives that hold our energy and give focus to the allurement that resides within us and draws us in. While the Universe Story flows from science and the Christian story from religious tradition, each is rooted in and attends to the dynamic and creative impulse at the heart of the cosmos. We can use different words, but at the core we are speaking of the single reality that is at our own core. We are the Universe Story. We are the Christian story. Language may vary, but the message is the same: we are here as the result of a single and radically amazing process that has involved eon upon eon of grace.

Images That Hold Our Energy: Morphogenic Fields and Holons

We have acknowledged the difficulty of holding the cosmic in a way that does not overwhelm us. The responses to the whale-sized crises of our time require cosmic consciousness, but our actions have to be local—in the here and now. Cosmology and theology give us the view, but in this unique moment in time we need something that will help us engage in the work.

It is helpful to have an image that helps contain our energy and imagination. As Bill Harris has noted, our mind interprets the image we hold as an invitation to make it happen. We move toward the object of our focus. I have proposed the image of the morphogenic field as a suitable one to engage our imagination and energy in ways that help us respond to the challenge that is ours.

A morphogenic field is a non-material region of influence around a system or holon or form. It helps hold the energy of a system, keeping it coherent. A morphogenic field is a field of information, memory, or habit and can be found at every level of existence, from atoms to individuals to groups. Each of us is a morphogenic field composed of smaller morphogenic fields and part of larger morphogenic fields. Each nonlocal field has its own quality of energy, its own region of influence. Each has its own distinct character and habits, its own particular feel, language, and way of doing relationships.

Morphogenic fields are sustained by morphic resonance, the influence of like upon like. Morphic resonance resembles a current of energy that flows into and helps sustain a morphogenic field, much like tributaries feed into the flow of a river. New morphogenic fields come into existence as they emerge from prior fields. While a new field may transcend an old one, the memory and therefore part of the energy that is resonant in the old is contained in the new. An emergent field may find resonance with many other fields, and the greater the number of fields with which it finds resonance, the stronger the emergent field will be. As the new field gains strength, its own morphic resonance increases and functions as an attractor, allowing others to enter the emergent field with greater ease. For example, those who now enter the field of computers, which many of us have struggled to comprehend over the past decades, will find learning those skills easier because of the memory, habits, and information that resonate within the now-established field.

As an image and as a reality, the morphogenic field holds energy that can help us connect to what is emerging in a coherent and tangible way. It functions as a container that holds our experience and focuses our attention, all the while allowing the energy of the field to strengthen and attract others.

Another name for a morphogenic field is "holon." Everything in the universe is a holon or whole/part. Nothing is a whole entirely unto itself, while nothing is a part separate from everything else. Everything is a whole/part. Each holon has four capacities: self-preservation, self-adaptation, self-transcendence, and self-dissolution.

Self-preservation refers to the capacity for autonomy or autopoiesis. It involves our ability to function as a whole, to live as a unique and gifted person who can be self-regulating and self-referring while maintaining integrity. It includes the way we live as subjects, the kind of sense of self that develops, as well as our power to assign meaning to that which we experience. Its key question is, "What will I do with my freedom?"

Self-adaptation is the capacity for relationship with others. We don't simply "have" relationships, we are relationship itself. We seek to connect with others, enjoying the synergy that comes when we join the whole self to the wholly other, discovering in the process that at our deepest roots there is no self and other, only a "we" that in its most pristine moments is celebrated in communion. The key question that surfaces as we exercise our capacity for self-adaptation is, "How do I connect with others?"

Self-transcendence refers to the holon's capacity to become more than it presently is. We are built to evolve. In each and every circumstance of our lives we are met with the invitation to transcend, to become more fully human, more capable of communion, more deeply free. Self-transcendence is that which urges us from within to engage the next question and to draw upon every resource we have in order to respond. At its core, the capacity for self-transcendence poses the question, "How do I choose to live? How will I go about the quest for knowledge, truth, and love?"

Self-dissolution is the fourth capacity of each holon. This element of our experience has to do with our resistance, as well as the acknowledgement that we are finite beings. At every moment that we experience the urgings of transcendence, we are also dying. The encroachment of physical death is a certainty, but we also experience the dyings that occur as we strive to transcend ego and give ourselves over to life on the cosmic scale. At its core the capacity for self-dissolution seeks to respond to the question, "How do I choose to die?" We must ask this question as comfortably as we ask all the others. Implicit in the response will be the affirmation of how we choose to live and what we choose to resist: "I will die for this, *not* this."

An understanding of the capacities of holons in connection with the image of morphogenic fields helps provide a focus for bringing together the various resonances that are contributing to the new morphogenic field—the new consciousness—that is emerging. The Universe Story, the Christian story, and the kingdom of God can be viewed as three distinct morphogenic fields, yet they share a common resonance. Each is fundamentally a story that speaks to the primacy of connectedness.

The Universe Story is one of cosmogenesis, a single creative event from which all life has emerged. The Christian story is one of connectedness as well. The creation event is interpreted as a single act of divine grace that is integral to the world as a whole, climaxing in a profound experience of unity in the Incarnation, an event in which divine revelation and human acceptance consummate. Within the Christian story the image of the kingdom of God proposes that the connectedness at the heart of all creation be lived out tangibly in the here and now in the relationships around us.

Each of the three morphogenic fields offers a cosmic view of the world. The perspective of each story can pull us out of egocentric absorption and into a panoramic view of the history of creation. In each narrative we are reminded that unity precedes diversity and that diversity seeks unity in the never-ending flow of communion. Each story acknowledges and calls forth the four capacities of holons. The Universe

Story itself is a story of the self-transcendence of the cosmos, of an endless process of becoming more, with each part being invited to preserve itself while entering into new relationships with all else. Death and dissolution are integral to the process and partner with life to allow the whole of creation to go on.

In the Christian story it is possible to see the Incarnation as the definitive affirmation of our capacity for transcendence, our movement toward the Holy, as well as the affirmation of our capacity for communion, together engaging our quest for truth and love and freedom in the material world. The kingdom of God reminds us that all of these capacities are not only rooted in matter, but must be lived in the material realm.

Emerging Capacities

The new consciousness did not arise in a vacuum, but has emerged from these and other life-giving stories or morphogenic fields that share the vision of connectedness of all that is. In earlier chapters we have looked at other morphogenic fields that we can engage because they affirm that our species is moving toward unitive consciousness and we have powerful tools at our disposal that allow us to participate more fully in the grace-filled process.

The work of Susanne Cook-Greuter is quite helpful because it shows us that the unitive consciousness once considered the purview of rare individuals is the kind of consciousness to which our species is evolving. With information based on empirical data, Cook-Greuter describes the emerging perspective on a large scale. Previously the characteristics of these stages of development have been expressed in religious terms. Indeed these stages are often the result of sustained attention to "religious experience" (experience of the transcendent), yet they may be described as profoundly "human experience," accessible through experience described as religious but not limited to any particular religious tradition. Since often the images and metaphors used in religious expression stem from a cosmology rooted in the Paleolithic era, their use has sometimes been as restrictive as it is liberating. Using the language of psychology allows us to move to a place of detachment from religious language so that we may update our own stories and images in a way that is resonant with the newer vision of reality that has been revealed. Far from separating us from our religious tradition, psychology can help us become clearer about what is of the essence.

The two higher stages examined by Cook-Greuter, Construct-Aware and Unitive, fall into the broader category of unitive consciousness. Individuals in these stages have developed the capacity to witness their own experience rather than be embedded in it. They have grown through the various developmental stages, with each stage becoming the object of the emerging stage. Both stages recognize the limitations of the ego and understand just how egocentric they have been. This recognition serves to free them of egocentricity and its concomitant illusions and to be vigilant with regard to the ego's ploys. They notice incongruities and paradoxes in their experience of the world, but they no longer see them as problems to be solved, but simply notice that they are part of the ongoing flow of life itself.

As they have moved through the stages, both Construct-Aware and Unitive adults have grown in their embrace, capable of including more and more of reality in their own worldview. They no longer consider themselves separate from the world but recognize that they are part of a single reality. While the Construct-Aware person may still experience a sense of separation between self and the world, the Unitive lives with a felt sense of connectedness to all that is. What the Construct-Aware knows, the Unitive has integrated more fully. Both view reality from deep time and deep space, recognizing that they are part of a process of cosmic proportions.

In light of the issues that threaten our very existence, it seems that to have a greater number of people in these higher stages of development, persons who have a sense of connectedness and who can embrace that reality in the way they live, contributes to the transformation in the consciousness of the whole. As it is lived on a larger scale, this level of consciousness shifts the center of gravity upward, pressuring the whole of our species to evolve.

While it is not possible to skip stages in the process of growth and development, it is possible to accelerate our movement through them with the practice of meditation. Sustained meditation facilitates changes within the brain. While one hemisphere of our brain usually predominates over the other, a phenomenon known as lateralization, the practice of meditation over time brings the hemispheres into balance. The result is that the sense of separation characteristic of lower stages of development begins to recede and a sense of connectedness begins to emerge.

Meditation loosens the hold that the ego has over consciousness and allows the subject of one stage to become the object of the next. It helps the person overcome inattentional blindness and facilitates ever larger views of the world. It trains the mind to witness, to disengage from thoughts and actions, and to observe without judgment. Meditation enables the practitioner to live in the present moment with an abiding state of peace, no matter what the external circumstances may be.

Meditation accelerates our growth into cosmic or unitive consciousness. Far from being an escape from reality, it hastens its embrace. Meditation is not for the faint of heart or the weak in spirit. The process is an arduous one, for it involves facing egocentricity, engaging the shadow, observing incongruities, spotting illusions, letting go of attachments, and monitoring the capacities for self-preservation, self-adaptation, self-transcendence, and self-dissolution. While it helps us grow and develop, it is not about acquiring any particular state or stage of consciousness as the endgame, but it is one way we may choose to engage evolutionary grace.

The point of meditating is not to become a meditator. The goal is not to reach a final state or stage of human development. Meditation and the evolution to a cosmic perspective simply prepare us for the work ahead. They hold us steady so that we may engage the whales. They teach us to employ our capacities to the fullest in ways that facilitate the evolution of all life. They help us live in the awareness of the connectedness that the Universe Story so beautifully demonstrates. They allow us to witness that life is wrapped in incomprehensible holy mystery and filled with grace. And they empower us to respond from a place that is free to love.

We are the universe come to consciousness. We are the universe awakened to its own empowerment. We know that every movement we make causes a shift of energy and ruffles the space around us. As Marianne Williamson has pointed out, we are powerful beyond measure. As we embrace that power we embrace the world, and as we embrace the world we begin to see that we must co-create, we must become instruments of the grace that everywhere abounds.

A promising tool at our disposal is the power of intention. Experiments have measured the physiological effects that come when we hold a particular intention for the purpose of healing. Studies suggest that more coherent energy influences the less coherent, that higher order influences the lesser. This begs the question that perhaps higher stages of consciousness—as powerful morphogenic fields that act as an attractor—can encourage lower stages to evolve more quickly. The phenomena of entrainment and resonance suggest that the more we vibrate at the same frequency, the stronger the field will become, the stronger the attraction will become, and the greater ease with which the field may be entered. Intentions held by small but pulsating groups can change energy patterns all over the globe. This is an awesome power, one we must not engage frivolously. As Lynne McTaggart points out, we are setting intentions all the time, usually unconsciously. What if we were to be intentional about our intentions, allowing them to come from the greatest depth we know?

Of course, the power of intention can be misused. If it is the case that we are always setting intentions anyway, simply as the result of our thinking processes, then we must disengage from the inattentional blindness that has been there all along. We have set intentions unaware, inadvertently misusing a power that we did not know was ours. How do we learn to set healthy intentions? How do we set intentions that flow from the deep self and not a fear-filled ego? We meditate. We become intentional about our own journey, and we share with others who do the same. We do not seek to arbitrarily establish our own morphogenic fields, but pay close attention to that which is emerging as a result of the pressure of the Spirit and then do what we can to grow in wisdom and respond with grace.

We are prepared for the call that is ours. We have all the tools required to step into the stream of grace-filled consciousness that is ours to live. The journey will be messy. We will miss a few steps and we will not always make the best of choices, but journey we must—together—growing all the while in our capacity to become people of compassion.

A CONTEMPLATIVE PAUSE

Settle into a quiet inner space, take a few deep relaxing breaths, and then, when you are ready, enter into the following exercises.

- I consider insights within me that have come throughout this chapter. Where is there resonance? Where is there resistance? Where is the realignment?

- I spend a moment simply gazing at the big picture that has emerged in this chapter. I look at the whole and attend to what is moving in me.

- I allow myself to be drawn in to one or more of the details. What is emerging in me as a result?

- I examine my capacity for hope. How hopeful am I—and for what do I hope?

A PRAYER

Holy Mystery, for eons you have prepared our species for this moment in time. Beginning as inert matter, all creation has evolved age on age, until at last we have become conscious of ourselves. In my personal life I can witness my own evolution in consciousness, my own coming to awareness of the grace and power you have given. Just as you have prepared our species, you have prepared me for this moment in time. May I not fail to engage the gifts you have given, may I use them generously in behalf of others, and together may we participate in the process of co-creation. Amen.

chapter
ten

A Field of Compassion

Only God could say what this new spirit gradually forming within you will be. Give our Lord the benefit of believing that His Hand is leading you, and accept the anxiety of feeling yourself in suspense and incomplete.

Pierre Teilhard de Chardin

The challenge now is to create an entirely new, vital revolution that takes the whole of life into its sphere. We have never dared embrace the whole of life in all its awesome beauty; we've been content to perpetuate fragments, invent corners where we feel conceptually secure and emotionally safe. . . . Today . . . we can no longer go on with this game of fragmentation.

Vimala Thakar

Compassion is the radicalism of our time.

The Dalai Lama

For the past few years I have facilitated week-long retreats as well as days of reflection that engage the subject of morphogenic fields. I usually begin the session by asking participants to imagine that the new human being—one with cosmic or unitive consciousness—has already arrived on planet Earth. Each participant is asked to compile a list of words, phrases, or images that describe the new person. What characteristics will be both descriptive and essential? What will relationships look like? How will institutions look, and what will they be about? What will life on planet Earth look like when the new consciousness takes hold?

After each person's list is complete, small groups of four to six are invited to share, noticing in their conversation where there is repetition and where a more complete picture emerges as a result. Finally, each small group captures the essence of their discussion on large newsprint, then shares their reflection with the entire group. After all the groups share with one another, I repeat many of the words spoken— and then tell participants that the words they have just spoken have been repeated all over the world. In gatherings from Cleveland to Oakland, from London in Ontario to Ty Croeso in Wales, with participants from India and Ireland, South America and Africa and everywhere in between, there has come a resonant response. The words and images are repeated time after time with the same conviction and with an assurance that these characteristics must be engaged for the sake of our species and our planet.

To me the repetition suggests that the new human being and its morphogenic field have already emerged. We cannot name with such precision something that is too far beyond our grasp. We have begun to know the depth of our capacities—we simply do not yet understand how to fully engage them. We are like nomads standing at the brink of a promised land, hearing the command to choose life, wanting to choose life, yet knowing that this is a learn-as-you-go venture.

The characteristics of the emerging human consciousness are not startlingly new. They flow out of the old and have been part of our consciousness for a very long time. Yet now they are named and spoken with a newfound conviction and urgency, because the time we have for turning the whales is running out.

The characteristics so often named include love, care, compassion, freedom, courage, unity, simplicity, solidarity, belonging, diversity, empowerment, harmony, equality, and hope. Images that keep repeating are the circle, the spiral, and the dance. The new human is intuitive, has a sense of the whole, lives with integrity, has the ability to make sacrifices on behalf of the whole, is discerning, and takes risks. Relationships are based on mutuality and respect and genuine concern for the common good and are inclusive of everyone, including Earth itself. The new human is both prophet and mystic. The prophet is engaged in the material world, sees with great clarity, and calls the species to grace. The mystic is engaged in the transcendent world, drawn toward incomprehensible holy mystery and unafraid of grace. But far from being separate engagements, the prophetic and mystic roles entangle and have a unitive flow about them.

As I have reflected on these elements and the way they are repeated time after time, I have also noticed how well they resonate with the four capacities of holons. Obviously each and every characteristic of the new consciousness is the result of self-transcendence—of the universe, of the human species, of the human person. In a sense, the evolution of the cosmos, an act of divine grace, meets itself in a deeper way in this new place. Human acceptance and divine outpouring meet a little more fully here. And the acceptance is not merely the assent to a belief that grace-filled outpouring has occurred, it is—it must be—the full acceptance of the power and energy of the grace that we are.

The new human who manifests a Field of Compassion not only receives grace but becomes grace. Once we enflesh it, we join with the Holy as co-creators who manifest grace in the world. It is not that we have never done this before—we are always living, breathing manifestations of grace. But most of the time we have been unaware, and awareness, clarity of vision, and the ability to focus—these are essential as we enflesh grace consciously in this moment of cosmic history. This work is at the heart of our capacity for self-transcendence; indeed, it is the fulfillment of self-transcendence itself in our time and in our day.

It is subjects who transcend, who become more open, conscious, and free. That is why the new human holon will engage all its capacity to be a whole. If an atom collapses and is no longer a whole atom, it cannot participate in the life of molecules. It cannot transcend. The same applies to us. We cannot participate in the more complex if we are not a whole. And, of course, none of us is completely whole—we cannot be, because we are participants in evolution. But we can become whole enough. That's all. Just whole enough, open enough for the Holy to work with us.

It seems then that commitment to a path that helps us become whole is essential. The autonomous subject must continue to grow in increasing embrace, slipping past egocentricity and coming to stand in a sense of self that is rooted in the sacred ground of all being. The new human needs to live in integrity—integrating each experience in a way that fosters increasing embrace. Living out of the stance of witness is crucial, for it teaches us that we are not our thoughts or feelings or experiences—we are something far and from beyond.

The more whole we are, the more vital will be our relationships. We will bring into our being with others a sense of self in which egocentric need is diminished and the ability to connect whole-to-whole is possible. I think this is perhaps where the life of Jesus is so helpful for us. We see the wholeness in his strength, conviction, and courage. He never seemed to relate to others except from a place of integrity, mutuality, and love. He taught with an authority that came from the knowledge of the Holy Unity, not from any need to control. Those who listened and were caught by his message responded authentically—because he himself was authentic.

The relationships characteristic of the new human are therefore subject-to-subject. The other is not really other, but simply a simultaneous and concomitant expression of grace itself. The new human is a "we," but one grounded in a whole "me." In the mystery of the communion experience—as "me" and "we" come together in sacred space—duality falls away and we find ourselves part of the sacred unity that is the heartbeat of the universe.

What brings our capacity for self-transcendence, self-preservation, and self-adaptation into focus is our capacity for self-dissolution. We are truly frail creatures, each breath contingent. The next breath is never a certainty, and the final breath will come sooner than we care to imagine. The gift of self-dissolution is that it challenges us to face our fear. Perhaps more than anything else, the experience of self-dissolution invites us to engage what we have learned. The new human enters this space by choice and witnesses the encroachment of all our dyings with freedom.

The hallmark of our new consciousness is freedom, for it is only from a place of freedom that we can be people of compassion. Only someone who is free can turn away from the whining of the ego and engage life fully. We cannot be whole if we are not free. We cannot enter fully into communion if we are not free. But when we are free, we encourage others to be free. Freedom is as contagious as fear; it just sometimes seems that we are not exposed to it often enough.

The morphogenic Field of Compassion is here. It is now. People all over the world have witnessed its coming. We can recognize it, describe it, and begin to live it with intention. We have wonderful tools at our disposal—and we now have each other. Together we walk into a consciousness not yet mapped—but we know we can as one hold the whales and allow our energy to transform the world.

A CONTEMPLATIVE PAUSE

Settle into a quiet inner space, take a few deep relaxing breaths, and then, when you are ready, enter into the following exercises.

- I consider insights within me that have come throughout this chapter. Where is there resonance? Where is there resistance? Where is the realignment?

- I list the characteristics that I intuitively know are part of the new human consciousness. I then identify these characteristics within my self and embrace each one.

- I examine my capacities of self-transcendence, self-preservation, self-adaptation, and self-dissolution, and then I notice what emerges. What needs my attention?

- I witness my capacity for freedom and compassion. How will I nurture these capacities, and how will I engage them today?

A PRAYER

Holy Unity, because of your gracious love, I share in the new consciousness that is emerging. What an awesome gift this is, that you have poured yourself out so generously. May I grow in all the capacities I have—in my self-transcendence, in autonomy, in communion, so that I may know who I am in you and who you are in me. And then, rooted in the knowledge of your love, may I walk freely and compassionately on earth. Amen.

chapter
eleven

Manifesting a Field of Compassion

We were made for something cosmic and will not fit peacefully into anything much smaller.

Matthew Fox

Compassion is the keen awareness of the interdependence of all things.

Thomas Merton

You may say that I'm a dreamer, but I'm not the only one.

John Lennon

Although I have discussed key elements of it, I have not yet precisely defined the Field of Compassion, this emerging new consciousness. That is intentional. My concern is inattentional blindness. If we define something as *this*, we may fail to notice *that*. Instead, in this chapter I would like to offer some observations that may help us walk this path together. We will begin with love.

The entire history of the universe has been the history of the outpouring of love. Karl Rahner reminded us that grace is nothing other than the Divine's self-communication in love. God creates in order to give God's self away in love. All that creation has ever been invited to do is accept this gift of love. Because of our unique consciousness, our human species has the capacity to receive this love in a wondrous way. Our species has the capacity to know that we are the result of God's self-expression. We can glimpse the depth of love that fashions us, we can recognize where we came from, and we can respond by allowing love entry. Unfortunately, in our orientation toward action, we have forgotten that we are merely receivers. Nothing we do can generate love. Perhaps this subtle distinction points to our greatest idolatry: to think that we are the lover rather than the loved. This is not to say that we do not love, but it is to remind us that we cannot love until we are loved. We are nothing more than conduits of divine love. We cannot give what we have not received.

Creation itself bears witness to the notion that love can only be understood fully when it is enfleshed in the material world and apprehended by material-spiritual beings. Choosing not to remain unexpressed, the Holy One created the material world and empowered it with the capacity for self-transcendence. In the world we know, tangibility has always been part of divine expression. Love has never been merely an abstraction but has been rooted in matter and articulated with substance. Love is not love until it is poured out into something or someone who has the capacity to receive it. Love is incomplete if it does not both offer and yield to embrace.

So much of the time we fret over relationships, asking ourselves how to love another. What can we do to show the other that we care? How can we move past hurt and move toward reconciliation? The answer is simple: receive the other's love. Many of us are blessed with all kinds of relationships in our lives, from family to workplace, from friends to communities. At some level we recognize these persons care about us, are pulling for us, hoping for us, intending what is life-giving for us—all expressions of love. Do we ever pause for a moment and simply receive their love? Doing so can be life-changing.

Receiving love brings us to a place of vulnerability. That is why it is so difficult. So often we live in the illusion that it is much easier to love than to be loved. We may think we can exercise a bit of control in loving another, but there is no control in being loved. The ones who truly love us walk into our hearts, often unnoticed, unannounced, and then reveal to us how genuinely loveable we are. And nothing feels more vulnerable than that. Nothing feels more vulnerable than allowing another access to who you are. Nothing feels more vulnerable than hearing words of kindness and care echo through your being. Being loved disarms us, brushes away our ego defenses, and then exposes us not only to the other, but to ourselves. And it is from ourselves that we most often hide our gaze. To see ourselves as we truly are—a wisp of love itself—is perhaps our deepest fear. But it is also our greatest grace. If we are to be the new human, we must begin by embracing love, which always seeks to incarnate itself. Love is enfleshed everywhere. Everywhere the Holy One is shouting and whispering, "Let me love you." And all that is asked of us is to receive. In reality, that is our life's work. Nothing more, and certainly nothing less.

Once we receive love, we become love. Once we learn to hold the love poured out through relationships and all the other parts of creation, we become love. Our very nature is changed. Could this be what Paul meant when he said, "Not

I now, but Christ lives in me"? Not I, but love received in me, love outpoured through me.

Love by its nature transforms. When we allow love in, we are transformed, and the love that we become then manifests in the world. When we resonate with love, when we are living, breathing vibrations of love energy, we contribute to the Field of Compassion, the new consciousness that is gracing the world.

Attitudes for Manifesting a Field of Compassion

There are four attitudes or stances that I think will help us enflesh the Field of Compassion on earth. They are essential postures from which we engage our capacities as holons. These attitudes grow and become more refined as we journey through the stages of development and engage in the practice of meditation. They are the places in which we can make the Universe Story and the Christian story real. They can help us respond tangibly and locally to the vast mystery beyond all we can imagine.

SPACIOUSNESS

The first attitude is *spaciousness*. The word "compassion" means literally "to suffer from the bowels." The image itself suggests not that I have entered into *your* space, but that I have allowed you to enter *my* space. This posture essentially says: "There is space for myself in you." There is a story told about the Hindu mystic Ramakrishna. One day as he was sitting quietly talking with his disciples, he suddenly fell to the floor and began to cry out in pain. Welts and bruises appeared on his body, and he was clearly in distress. One of his disciples ran out into the street—and there found one man beating another. "There is space in myself for you."

An attitude of spaciousness is a reflection of the Holy itself. Last summer I traveled with friends from Llantarnam Abbey in the south of Wales through Betws-y-coed toward the Snowden Mountains in the north. I remember clearly the turn onto the road to Llanberis. At the time, we were listening to a recording of the Treorchy Male Choir; at the moment the mountains opened up to our view, the men's voices rang out the "Hallelujah!" from Wagner's "Pilgrim's Chorus." I was so overcome by the beauty of the experience that tears began to stream down my face. What I sensed in this moment was the spaciousness of the Holy One, the immensity of God's heart and the breadth of divine love. That is the spaciousness from which we come, and it is the spaciousness with which we encounter the other. "There is space in myself for you."

CONTEMPLATION

The second posture that is essential as we live the Field of Compassion is *contemplation*. I do not mean a particular kind of prayer, but rather an orientation toward life itself. An old definition of contemplation is "taking a long, loving look at the real." It involves attending to what is before us, free from inattentional blindness. Contemplation means that we are aware of what is before us, awakened to possibilities that are around us—seeing what we see, hearing what we hear, as if for the first time, fresh, without prejudice.

One of my greatest lessons in contemplation came from my younger son Doug when he was just a little over a year old. One evening he came padding into the living room, clad only in a diaper and undershirt, grabbed my hand, and pulled me into the bedroom. He ran over to the window and pointed up. "Moon," he said. "Moooon!" It was a windy night. Clouds covered the moon and then quickly swept away, and Doug thought the moon was playing peek-a-boo with us. He sat on my lap, then popped up in delight as the silver orb came into sight again. He gasped in disbelief and jumped with delight. For an hour we watched the spectacle of an autumn sky. In the moment I realized how long it had been since I had really looked at the moon, how long it had been since I had given a long, loving look at what is real. Grateful for my little son's teaching, I have never forgotten that moment.

A contemplative stance is the fruit of meditation. It allows us to live out of the witness, the place where we learn to let our thoughts and feelings pass by, becoming attached to nothing, becoming identified with nothing. This stance is where we are most free, unfettered by fear and unhindered by ego. By allowing us to stand back and see what is real, contemplation helps us to spot our attachments and our illusions—and once we spot them, we can be free from them.

In the Hasidic tradition there is a saying that goes: "Each person is surrounded by a legion of angels proclaiming 'Behold the image of God.'" Only contemplative seeing can do that kind of beholding. Contemplation allows us to see how connected we are to all that is, and that is the essence of mysticism. Karl Rahner said that the Christian of the future will be a mystic or nothing at all. I think our generation can revise that statement to say that the human being of the future will be a mystic or nothing at all. What is a mystic? Simply the one who sees that there is only the One reality. The mystic experiences the essence of the Universe Story and the Christian story: everything is connected, and all is one.

COMMITMENT

A third attitude that will enable us to enflesh the Field of Compassion is *commitment*. Our lives can be about so many trivial things. We can get swept away by the superficial and peripheral. We can bow to our ego and cave in to our fear. And we can do so mindlessly, allowing our lives to slip by with very little meaning. In the act of commitment, both our focus (our mind moves toward the image we hold) and our intention come together in a tangible way. Focus and intention maintain the morphic resonance that sustains the morphogenic field.

One of the most powerful stories that I have heard about commitment, focus, and intention came from John Dear's web site a few years ago. It seems that in the 1980s a small group of people gathered in a church basement in East Germany to engage the question: "What will Germany be like a thousand years from now when the Berlin Wall finally falls?" At the time that notion seemed an utter impossibility. The country was rooted in communism, in the iron-clad grip of the Soviet Union. And yet these folks engaged the question: "What will Germany be like a thousand years from now when the Berlin Wall finally falls?"

According to the story, the group felt energized by the discussion and agreed to meet again. Word of their gathering spread, and soon church basements all over Germany were filled with those who dreamed of unity and reconciliation. Over the next few years, a grassroots movement grew. Ordinary people met, prayed, organized. They committed their minds and hearts to the dream. Then in 1987, seemingly out of the blue, Mikhail Gorbachev announced the economic reforms known as *perestroika*. In Poland the Solidarity Movement pushed the Soviet Union out, and a new democracy was born. One event followed the next, and on November 9, 1989—much sooner than a thousand years—the Berlin Wall came down.

In the context of our discussion we can say that the effort of a very few who dared to dream created a morphogenic field. The field was sustained by the energy of focus and intention, and the more that energy increased, the more people joined in, the more the field resonated with power and strength. Human beings dared to engage what they most deeply knew to be true—that unity and reconciliation, peace and love, are what we are intended to manifest. We are given the grace, but we must participate in the unfolding. We are pressured from within to become all that we are. We yield to that pressure and receive what it offers. We engage it in freedom and love. And that transforms the world. Can we make any more significant commitment than this?

Like those who engaged the question about life after the Berlin Wall, we engage the questions—the whales—of our day and hold the image that carries the dream of wholeness. Theirs was not a commitment to revolution, although revolution occurred. It was not an engagement of purely political tactics, although the political climate changed. They were not about a campaign that promoted a particular ideology, even as the highest ideas of the people came to the fore. Real transformation occurred because the time was ripe, and what helped make the time ripe was the morphogenic field that emerged as they held to the vision. The field was sustained by morphic resonance—the energy of ordinary people who carried within themselves an extraordinary dream. And isn't that who we are?

IMAGINATION

The fourth posture that we must engage is our *imagination*. So often we say, "It was *only* my imagination." It is perhaps more proper to say, "It is *always* the imagination." All that is comes from divine imagination, and our capacity to envision that which does not exist and invite it to take form is one of our greatest gifts. It is our imagination that allows us to give form to the Spirit's urgings. We are able to imagine a Field of Compassion not because the vision originates with us. The dream originates in God, and through our imaginations we see it. We see whales turn and walls crumble. And as we see it, it becomes real. Our imaginations help us maintain the vision within ourselves, calling forth our creativity and commitment in the space that we provide them.

In Toni Morrison's novel *Beloved,* there is a character by the name of "Baby Suggs, holy." She is the grandmother of a troubled family of former slaves who live in Cincinnati, Ohio, in the decades after the Civil War. Baby Suggs, holy, is a preacher of sorts, and sometimes she delivers what seems to be her own sermons on the mount. One day when she is about to teach again, she gathers the children and the men and the women together. She asks the children to laugh. She asks the men to dance. She asks the women to cry for the living and the dead. But along the way it all gets mixed up, and in the end the women dance, the men cry, the children laugh, until finally all lay in an exhausted heap at Baby Suggs' feet. Then Morrison writes:

> In the silence that followed, Baby Suggs, holy, offered up to them her great big heart.
> She did not tell them to clean up their lives or to go and sin no more. She did not tell them they were the

blessed of the earth, its inheritance meek or its glory-
bound pure.
She told them that the only grace they could have was
the grace they could imagine. That if they could not see
it, they would not have it.[1]

The only grace we can have is the grace we can imagine.
If we cannot see it, we cannot engage it. If we cannot engage
it, we cannot manifest it, we cannot be the co-creators we
are invited to be. The morphogenic field we can have is the
one we can imagine. The Field of Compassion we envision
is the one that will manifest. Of course we remain open to
surprise, to pressure that invites us to look at something we
have not seen before. But all of our capacities as holons, all
the hallmarks that make us human—our quest to know, our
ability to be loved and be free—prepare us to participate in
the divine dream that we experience as a world of grace.

Spaciousness, contemplation, commitment, and imagination—cultivating these four stances will help us hold and
engage the energy required to manifest and maintain a Field
of Compassion. They help us first of all receive and hold love
that pours itself out for us. They tell us how to be, so that
truth may emerge. They engage all our capacities as holons,
as free subjects who are deeply graced. As each attitude
becomes integrated, as we ourselves become more spacious,
more contemplative, more committed to the work, and more
imaginative in our approach, a Field of Compassion emerges
and transforms us—and transforms the world.

A CONTEMPLATIVE PAUSE

Settle into a quiet inner space, take a few deep relaxing breaths, and then, when you are ready, enter into the following exercises.

- I consider insights within me that have come throughout this chapter. Where is there resonance? Where is there resistance? Where is the realignment?

- Try this exercise: sit quietly and bring to mind those who care for you—in the present and in the past. As you recall each person, receive the love that is there for you. Let it into your heart. Even if someone has a quirky way of showing love, receive the love. Sift through the dysfunction if you have to, but receive the love. Never mind if the person has never said, "I love you." Receive the love, one by one. Hold all that love in your heart. Let it penetrate your whole being. How does it feel to consciously, intentionally receive all of that love? Can you allow that to sustain your journey for today?

- What dream is taking form in you? What morphogenic field, what capacities of your holon-self are wanting to manifest in a new way? Contemplate that which is emerging and image the grace unfolding in and through your life. Remember that the only grace you can have is the grace you can imagine. If you cannot see it, you will not have it.

A PRAYER

Holy Heart of the Universe, you call us to dream, to imagine, to yield to your grace, your pressure from within to evolve. Help us to see that all that we are has come about through the 13.7-billion-year unfolding of your grace. Help us to grasp the reality that the entire history of the universe has prepared us to be the ones who enflesh your imagination in the material world. May we celebrate who we are as we celebrate who you are, and may we dare to imagine that we are grace itself. Amen.

chapter
twelve

Engaging the Grace
We Imagine

*Our worst fear is not that we are inadequate, our deepest
fear is that we are powerful beyond measure. It is our light,
not our darkness that most frightens us.*

Marianne Williamson

*Today, as we take risks
for the sake of something greater
than our separate, individual lives,
we are feeling graced by other beings and by Earth itself.*

Joanna Macy

In the early morning hours after Jesus' crucifixion, Mary
Magdalene, Mary, the mother of James, and Salome, laden
with spices for anointing, set out for the burial place of their
beloved. As they made their way, the concern was the heavy
stone that sealed the tomb, an obstacle much too heavy for

them to move alone. But when they arrived they encountered something completely unexpected. The stone had been rolled away, and the tomb was empty save for a messenger who said that Jesus was raised and no longer there. This discovery so terrified the women that they ran away in fear.

It is easy to understand their fright. Resurrection is simply another image for new awareness, is it not? Resurrection is a quantum leap in complexity and consciousness, brought about by an experience of grace that is permanent and life-changing. It yanks us out of the comfortable and sets us in front of something that is totally unfamiliar. It is important that we remember this, because the call to inhabit a new morphogenic field and manifest a new consciousness is not a summons to anything superficial. Cosmic change is not cosmetic change. It is radical, meaning "to the root," and it will mean the upheaval of our cherished customs and the disposal of stories that have provided the basic framework for our lives. We must not underestimate the enormity of what is being asked of us, even as we celebrate with joy the new and salvific.

In its initial moments resurrection is indistinguishable from death. At first we are unable to see the great turning that has taken place. All that has been comfortable, all that has held us in place is gone, and there is nothing recognizable to stand on. Everything on which we have planted our feet is swept away. In this context resurrection is as much self-dissolution as it is self-transcendence, and we can be tempted to respond passively to these experiences, allowing them to run over us and push us into egocentric fear and victimhood. But we must recognize that even here—especially here—we are called to engage all our capacities as human holons.

For many years I have embraced the words written by Marianne Williamson: "Our worst fear is not that we are inadequate, our deepest fear is that we are powerful beyond measure. It is our light, not our darkness that most frightens us."[1] It is resurrection, not death, that is most terrifying. More than the cessation of life, it is the embrace of new power that surfaces our deepest fears. The distinction is quite subtle, but it is significant. In the experience of resurrection, we discover that self-transcendence and self-dissolution are friends, and the simultaneous engagement of both capacities is required for our emergence into new consciousness.

I often think of the chrysalis as it awakens to being the butterfly. There is the silent and soft unfolding, the moments of fragile, wet vulnerability, and, after some time, the ever-so-slight movement of wings. Surely the butterfly does not know that its barely perceptible ruffle can alter an energy pattern on the other side of the globe. It simply goes about being a butterfly, living with its own kind of integrity the holon that it is, sustained by the morphogenic field of its species. But to get to this place, it had to die.

Death is the prerequisite for the experience of resurrection and the new freedom it brings. At some level, in some way, perhaps far beyond our conscious awareness, we must first assent to dying. Resurrection—the emergence of new consciousness—is an awakening to the unknown, and just as with any other experience of life that is unknown, it can be frightening. We intuitively know that everything has changed, and if we are the kind of person who is attached to safety and comfort, we will feel overwhelmed. We may very well run, just as Mary Magdalene and the other women did. But the new day had already come, and as dawn turned to daylight and daylight passed to evening, these first disciples gradually awakened to what had happened. Fragile and vulnerable, in a soft and silent place in their hearts, they awakened to not only the resurrection of Jesus, but to the resurrection of themselves. I have no doubt that they returned to the tomb, and the symbol that had initially marked a terrifying moment filled with fear became a monument to the most inexpressible of gift of Spirit.

The knowledge that our species has gained over the last several decades has revealed to us both the immensity and intricacy of our cosmos, and it has brought us to an experience of resurrection—of new consciousness that alters everything. Whether we use scientific language or religious language, the story that expresses what we have learned is one of connectedness. We know we are part of a grand and grace-filled whole. And we know that in spite of the scientific precision or images that seek to express the ineffable, our words are always limp, always fall short of what we intend to convey, because our understanding, in all its sophistication, is so very, very incomplete. The mystery from which we come allows us only a glimpse at this point in our evolution. Our holding capacity is not yet spacious enough to embrace it all. But as we enter into each resurrection experience, as we simultaneously embrace self-transcendence and self-dissolution, our capacity to hold just a little more mystery expands, and in the experience we embrace a little more of who we are.

The Grace We Can Imagine

The only grace we can have is the grace we can imagine. Implied in Morrison's words is the acknowledgment of our human responsibility to participate in the unfolding of the universe. We are the universe come to consciousness. We are the ones who can recognize that we live in a world of grace and that grace itself is our essence. We began with the story of the rescue of the whales. There are all sorts of whales in our lives—and some of them are big surprises.

I had just begun the tenth chapter of this book when I learned that a mass removed from my back was cancerous. I was stunned by the diagnosis, having had no expectation of hearing the words the surgeon spoke to me that afternoon. I felt well, and there were no signs that anything within my body was so amiss. By 8:00 the next morning, my husband and I were sitting in the oncologist's office, trying to take in new words and a very new reality. I learned that the cancer that had metastasized to an area on my back was originally from somewhere else in my body and that in 90 percent of cases they do not discover the originating site. I was told that the whole affair was "concerning."

The first two days I felt as if I had been hit hard in the gut, and it was difficult to take in all the information and its implications. But I remember that at some point on Monday afternoon, just a few hours after hearing the results of the pathology report, I realized that I did not feel any different physically than I had earlier in the day—before I had heard the news. I knew that the situation was serious, that because of the diagnosis I was looking at the possibility of death or at best some pretty serious medical interventions that would leave me feeling quite ill. But in truth I felt no different than I had that morning, except for the knot in the pit of my stomach.

I knew in that moment that I had a choice to make about how I would enter this unpredictable and unknown place. I knew also that my choice was only for this moment, for in such a wild place, choices can be made only for the moment. In this moment I would choose to enter the experience as consciously as possible. With divine grace and the supportive energy of family, friends, and community, I would try to remain in the place of witness and make every effort not to be ruled by fear. It seemed quite clear that this was the place where I must engage everything I had ever learned.

Of course I cried. I wept from a place very deep within. There was so much life I had yet to experience, so many loving relationships I did not want to let go of. And I knew that I could die. As I continued to stay with what was going on in me over those first few days, I recognized that my greatest fear was not my own death. My greatest fear was that I would fail to live this moment of my life with integrity. Since all that I have written is what I hold to be true at the core of my being, I knew that this was the moment of truth for me, and I was staking my life on all the words that had been pouring out day after day.

Since the new consciousness is characterized by both "me" and "we," I began by sending a message to two of my community groups within the Congregation of St. Joseph. Part of our commitment to one another is to share how we see the Spirit moving in our personal lives, and so my first act after telling family was to share my heart with those who I knew would listen without trying to deny the reality or fix the feelings, who could support me best simply by holding me in good energy. Even though it is natural to feel fear for those we love, it was important for me to know that the prayers of those around me were not rooted in fear of my death, but rather flowed from energy that would facilitate healing and life. This was the request that I made: "Please, do not hold me in the energy of fear, but in the energy of healing intention and light." In that moment I felt healthy and my energy was good, and I experienced myself as a "we." That knowing held me in a place of peace and assurance—not of the outcome, but of the grace that would be there no matter what.

Meditation teaches us that we are not our thoughts, we are not our feelings, we are not our experiences. It allows us to assume the stance of witness, observing the flow of life without attachment and without judgment. I have practiced meditation over many years, and now I know for certain just how powerful—and life-saving—the discipline can be. I can tell you that I have had lots of thoughts and feelings throughout this experience, and what has helped most is the practice itself. I am engaged, some days painfully so, but continue to make the effort to work back to a degree of non-attachment in the moment. All of this, I know, is grace. What has been affirmed is that who I am—who each of us is—is far more profound than what we experience or what we have been told. This I know.

The six-month period after the initial diagnosis was difficult, to say the least. I have had many ups and downs, and those who say that the experience of cancer is a roller-coaster have just the right image. Not only are there highs and lows, but there are sudden twists in unexpected directions that require hanging on for dear life and leave you feeling bumped and bruised. There are in-between moments where you catch your breath just a little, then the intensity picks up again and all you can hope for is that the ride stops soon. As I write these words, the therapies have been completed, but I will be watched carefully over the next few months and years. While I do not yet know what the future holds, I know the process will continue to be filled with grace—because that is who mystery is and what mystery does.

I spent time re-reading these words during the weeks of medical treatment and the uncertainty that was part of it all. Of course, now I have read them from a consciousness that is different from the one in which I wrote them. I made no substantial changes because I continue to hold them as expressions of truths that have emerged over my lifetime. From this place, however, I have a few additional things to say.

Perhaps the most freeing insight that has come in the last few months is that it is helpful to throw away "beliefs." To me beliefs tend to be mental constructs, assertions *about* reality, not reality itself. My beliefs have tended to come from my head, not my heart. They are accompanied by rules and regulations—and not far behind comes judgment. As of right now, I find no comfort in any belief. What does sustain me is what I know to be true—perhaps not ultimate truth, but my truth, what I know in my heart. I know love, and love never seeks to separate or exclude. I know freedom, and freedom never lets ego and fear have the final say. I know I am not alone, that we are all connected in the web of life, and we feel the connection most powerfully when we operate from within a Field of Compassion. Certainly I am supported by what is of the essence of our tradition. I know Jesus, the human and the Christ, and I know a bit of mystery, and what I experience in that relationship is more powerful than any belief or idea. So I have kicked out beliefs in favor of holding what has emerged for me as true.

Without beliefs to uphold, I find that the temptation to judge begins to fall away. Each time I have judged, especially when I have thought something to be "wrong," I can track the judgment back to a belief—something more rooted in my head and unconsciousness than in my heart and compassion. By endeavoring to let go of judgment, my heart becomes more open to the flow of divine love. Ego gets out of the way a little more, and then love can flourish.

I have given more thought to our capacity to form and hold intentions. If our intentions were the bottom line, then I would be rid of cancer, simply because so many are holding the intention that I be whole and well. But it is not that simple. I know that in this most loving intention—one that I have requested and prayed for myself—there is a deeper mystery at work. At the moment my ego is very attached to this earthly life, but the work of incomprehensible holy mystery is graciously unbound by even the most well-intentioned ego. So we must remember that while it is our responsibility to participate co-creatively in evolution, the process itself is a mystery, ultimately outside our capacity to hold or understand.

This experience has affirmed the significance of the practice of meditation. Even now I know that I am not my feelings, I am not my thoughts, I am not even my experience. Who I am—who each of us is—is a much deeper mystery. We are so much, much more than we have believed we are. The practice of meditation teaches us to move back to the place of witness—and it teaches us that even when we cannot get back there, when all we can do is rage or weep or want to run away—that all is indeed well. No judgment—just the effort to love what is.

I am more certain than ever that the new consciousness is a "we." None of us can hold the really deep life experiences alone. The group that I call my "wisdom circle" met recently. There are seven of us women who gather and try to put words on and live out of the new consciousness in our daily lives. We admit that we are really on unbroken ground, territory that is unknown, yet we seek to live out what we sense is emerging and share the stories of our lives from that perspective. As I shared what was happening at this moment of my life, one of the women asked if I wanted to be touched. Without hesitation I said, "Yes," and they gathered around, praying, stroking, allowing my assaulted body to receive some tenderness. I cried—I think we all did—as I soaked in their love. The spontaneous image that came to me was a litter of puppies, all crawling over and leaning against one another. The close physical contact was nourishing, and the image sustained me in the days and weeks ahead. This experience of "we" gave energy to what I would be required to face alone.

The experience of "we" has also come from those who were not physically present but who continued day after day to hold me in healing light. Often I sat and simply imagined their love soaking into every cell of my body, cleansing, healing, allowing every piece of me to light up. Definitely, tangibly, the Field of Compassion is a "we."

In the introduction I wrote, "Life to the full is possible—but not without our choosing it one small action at a time." I am learning that as we choose, one small movement at a time, that fullness of life truly comes. The fullness may not be fluffy; it may be very, very difficult, but in some way each choice moves us more deeply into mystery, our origin and our home.

Our whales come in many guises, both collective and personal. But however they come, they offer the possibility of new consciousness and a deeper freedom than we ever dreamed we could have. Whether or not we evolve from the experience depends on our response. Truly the only grace we can have is the grace we can imagine, and our acts of imagination that really matter—the acts that grant us co-creative grace—come from the place of witness that allows us to form life-giving intentions. When we live this way, we inhabit a Field of Compassion that is so real, so tangible, so alluring, so vibrating with energy that others are drawn in, set free, and transformed. We all become filled with grace and the awesome recognition that incomprehensible holy mystery seeks to deliver itself into our hands.

What I also recognized along the way is that this chapter cannot be completed. In the writing I feel that I have simply been a conduit, writing words that originate beyond my own consciousness. The words are not something I own, even though I seek to live them with all my heart. The words are "ours," and they become true only if enough of us engage what the Spirit is trying to tell us not only here, but in every place we look with contemplative eyes. The new consciousness asks each of us to be a whole, an open and awake "me" that is the prerequisite for being the new "we." It is together that we move forward, listening to the incomprehensible holy mystery who is inviting us to live a new story, to embrace new powers, and to manifest a morphogenic field that will change the course of human history.

We are one, grounded in the 13.7-billion-year history of the universe. We have evolved as species and as individuals to this moment in time, a moment in which we are asked to engage not only the whales but the new powers that are ours. This is a moment of resurrection, and as we begin to live this new consciousness day after day after day, the whole world will be transformed. That is not a matter of thinking too much of ourselves, but a matter of accepting who we are in God and who God is in us.

We live in a world of grace, and as we more consciously receive grace, each of us becomes a Field of Compassion. Each one of us becomes open to love a little more completely, and then love pours out of us and into the world. As we become free, others experience freedom in our presence and can choose to be open to love, too. This is our life work, our great work, what the Universe asks and what this moment in time demands. Our work requires all that we have become and all that we are becoming. It requires a "yes" that at one moment may be whole-hearted and the next tentative and unsure. But together our "yes" is empowering. Let us imagine the grace, then, hold it in our hearts, and manifest, one day at a time, a Field of Compassion.

A CONTEMPLATIVE PAUSE

Settle into a quiet inner space, take a few deep relaxing breaths, and then, when you are ready, enter into the following exercises.

- I consider insights within me that have come throughout this chapter. Where is there resonance? Where is there resistance? Where is the realignment?

- I gaze contemplatively at the place of self-transcendence/ self-dissolution in my life that invites me to transformation.

- In this moment, I choose . . .

A PRAYER

Incomprehensible Holy Mystery, in and through your grace I can hold the gift of this moment in time. Help me embrace each and every resurrection, every experience of self-transcendence and self-dissolution that invites me to enflesh compassion and love in the world. May I continue to grow in my capacity to witness so that I may form intentions that are life-giving for all. May I engage the new story of connectedness in a way that facilitates my own evolution and calls others to evolve as well. May we together manifest a Field of Compassion, a place where the holy and human converge in grace. Amen.

Notes

Chapter One: The Significance of Story

1. Bill Harris, *Thresholds of the Mind* (Beaverton, OR: Centerpointe Press, 2002), 129. Used with permission of Centerpointe Research Institute, www.centerpointe.com. 800-945-2741.
2. David Bohm, quoted in Danah Zohar, *The Quantum Self: Human Nature and Consciousness Defined by the New Physics* (New York: William Morrow, 1990), 58.
3. Zohar, *The Quantum Self*, 36.
4. Ian Marshall and Danah Zohar, *Who's Afraid of Schrödinger's Cat?: An A-to-Z Guide to All the New Science Ideas You Need to Keep Up with the New Thinking* (New York: William Morrow, 1997), 77–78.
5. Ibid., 258.
6. Lynne McTaggart, *The Intention Experiment* (New York: Free Press, 2007), xiii.

Chapter Two: Morphogenic Fields

1. Paul A.M. Dirac, quoted in Benjamin Crowell, *Newtonian Physics* (Fullerton, CA: Light & Matter, 2000), 193.
2. Rupert Sheldrake, *The Presence of the Past: The Habits of Nature* (Rochester, VT: Park Street Press, 1995), 177–181; and Rupert Sheldrake, "Mind, Memory, and Archetype Morphic Resonance and the Collective Unconscious," *Psychological Perspectives* (Spring 1987), 18(1), 9–25.
3. Sheldrake, *The Presence of the Past*, 193–94.
4. A more complete description of morphogenic fields can be found in Rupert Sheldrake, *The Presence of the Past* and *A New Science of Life: The Hypothesis of Formative Causation*

(Los Angeles: J.P. Tarcher, 1981). A complementary description may be found in Judy Cannato, *Radical Amazement: Contemplative Lessons from Black Holes, Supernovas, and Other Wonders of the Universe* (Notre Dame, IN: Sorin Books, 2006).

5. Ibid., 99.
6. Ibid., 108.
7. Ibid., 109.
8. Ibid., 109.
9. Ibid., 115.
10. For a more detailed description of holons, consult Ken Wilber, *A Theory of Everything* (Boston: Shambhala Publications, 2000), or Judy Cannato, *Radical Amazement*, chapter 8.
11. Miriam Therese MacGillis, "Re-Visioning the Reign of God," essay.
12. Thomas Berry, *The Dream of the Earth* (San Francisco: Sierra Club Books, 1990), 106.
13. Elizabeth A. Johnson, *Quest for the Living God: Mapping Frontiers in the Theology of God* (New York: Continuum, 2007), 34.

Chapter Three: The Universe Story and Christian Story

1. Karl Rahner, *Foundations of Christian Faith: An Introduction to the Idea of Christianity*, William V. Dych, trans. (New York: Crossroad, 1993), 183.
2. Denis Edwards, *Jesus and the Cosmos* (New York/Mahwah: Paulist Press, 1991), 25.
3. Rahner, *Foundations of Christian Faith*, 183.
4. Ibid.
5. Ibid., 181.
6. Ibid., 182.
7. Ibid.
8. Ibid.
9. Ibid., 185–86.
10. Ibid., 189.

11. Karl Rahner and Herbert Vorgrimler, *Theological Dictionary*, Cornelius Ernst, O.P., ed., and Richard Strachan, trans. (New York: Herder and Herder, 1965), 465.

12. Rahner and Vorgrimler, *Theological Dictionary*, 158.

13. Rahner, *Foundations of Christian Faith*, 193.

14. Ibid., 181.

15. Ibid., 195.

16. Ibid.

17. Ibid.

18. Ibid., 194.

19. Ibid., 202.

20. Ibid.

21. Edwards, *Jesus and the Cosmos*, 69f.

22. Rahner, *Foundations of Christian Faith*, 194.

23. Jürgen Moltmann, *The Way of Jesus Christ: Christology in Messianic Dimensions*, Margaret Kohl, trans. (New York: HarperCollins, 1990), 73.

24. Rahner, *Foundations of Christian Faith*, 181.

25. Raimon Panikkar, *Christophany: The Fullness of Man*, Alfred DiLascia, trans. (Maryknoll, New York: Orbis Books, 2008), 150.

26. Rahner, *Foundations of Christian Faith*, 190.

27. Ibid., 181.

28. Elizabeth A. Johnson, *Consider Jesus* (New York: Crossroad, 1994), 123f.

Chapter Four: Morphic Resonance: Two Stories Converge

1. Michael Dowd, *Thank God for Evolution!* (San Francisco: Council Oak Books, 2007), 108.

2. John R. Sachs, S.J., *The Christian Vision of Humanity: Basic Christian Anthropology* (Collegeville, MN: The Liturgical Press, 1991), 61.

3. Ibid., 64.

4. Rahner, *Foundations of Christian Faith*, 111.

5. Ibid., 38.

Chapter Five: The "Kingdom of God"

1. Neil Douglas-Klotz, *The Hidden Gospel: Decoding the Spiritual Message of the Aramaic Jesus* (Wheaton, IL: Quest Books, 1999), 27.
2. Ibid., 35.
3. Beatrice Bruteau, *The Holy Thursday Revolution* (Maryknoll, NY: Orbis Books, 2005), 209.
4. Rahner and Vorgrimler, *Theological Dictionary,* 158.
5. Douglas-Klotz, *The Hidden Gospel,* 84.
6. Ibid.
7. Bruteau, *The Holy Thursday Revolution,* 207.

Chapter Six: Emerging Capacities

1. Susanne Cook-Greuter, "A Detailed Description of Nine Stages in Ego Development Theory Including the Construct-Aware and Unitive Stages," copyright 2005, Susanne Cook-Greuter, www.cook-greuter.com, 4.
2. Susanne Cook-Greuter, "Ego Development: Nine Levels of Increasing Embrace," 5. Prepublication document used by permission of the author. Susanne Cook-Greuter, www.cook-greuter.com.
3. Ibid.
4. Susanne Cook-Greuter, *Postautonomous Ego Development: A Study of Its Nature and Measurement* (Susanne Regina Cook-Greuter, 1999), 1. Dissertation presented to the Harvard University Graduate School of Education.
5. Cook-Greuter, "Ego Development," 29.
6. Ibid., 28.
7. Ibid.
8. Ibid.
9. Ibid., 29.
10. Ibid.
11. Ibid., 30.
12. Ibid.
13. Ibid., 31.
14. Ibid., 32.

15. Ibid.
16. Ibid.
17. Ibid., 32f.
18. Ibid., 33.
19. Ibid., 34.
20. Ibid.
21. Richard Rohr, "Utterly Humbled By Mystery," *National Catholic Reporter* interview, December 18, 2006.
22. Bill Harris, "Beyond the Separate Self: The Unitive Stage of Development" (Beaverton, OR: Centerpointe Press, 2008), 3. Used with permission of Centerpointe Research Institute, www.centerpointe.com. 800-945-2741.
23. Ibid., 5.

Chapter Seven: Meditation

1. One such account is given in *The New York Times*, "Science Watch: Heat from Meditation," February 9, 1982.
2. Harris, *Thresholds of the Mind*, 18.
3. Ibid.
4. Ibid., 18f.
5. Ibid., 21.
6. Ibid., 22.
7. Ibid., 19.
8. Ibid.
9. Ken Wilber, *Integral Spirituality: A Startling New Role for Religion in the Modern and Postmodern World* (Boston: Integral Books, 2006), 197.
10. Daniel J. Simons and Christopher F. Chabris, "Gorillas in Our Midst: Sustaining Inattentional Blindness for Dynamic Events," *Perception*, v. 28, 1999. 1059–74. The following web site allows you to view the video: http://viscog.beckman.uiuc.edu/grafs/demos/15.html.

Chapter Eight: The Power of Intention

1. Joelle Diderich, "Yanomami's Turn to Shamans to Stop Amazon Fires" (Reuters News Service, March 19, 1998) and "Shamans Called in to Fight Amazon Blaze" (Reuters

News Service, March 29, 1998); Anthony Faiola, "Watching Helplessly as Rain Forest Burns" (*Washington Post* Service, March 30, 1998); William Schomberg, "Rain Falls on Burning Amazon after Shaman's Ritual" (Reuters News Service, March 31, 1998) and "Rain Falls in Burning Amazon" (Reuters News Service, March 31, 1998).

2. Lynn McTaggart, *The Intention Experiment* (New York: Free Press, 2007), 8–10.
3. Ibid., xx.
4. Ibid., xxi.
5. Ibid., 23.
6. Ibid., 24.
7. Ibid.
8. Ibid., 27–30.
9. Ibid., 46.
10. Ibid., 47.
11. Ibid., 51.
12. Ibid., 52.
13. Ibid., 53.
14. Ibid., 54.
15. Ibid., 55.
16. It is possible to see the results of REG events as well as the current monitoring of events at http://gcpdot.com and http://noosphere.princeton.edu.
17. McTaggart, *The Intention Experiment*, 181.
18. Ibid., 185.
19. Ibid., 194.
20. The Energy Ball can be obtained from Educational Innovations, www.teachersource.com or 888-912-7474.

Chapter Eleven: Manifesting a Field of Compassion
1. Toni Morrison, *Beloved* (New York: Penguin Books, 1987), 88.

Chapter Twelve: Engaging the Grace We Imagine
1. Marianne Williamson, *A Return to Love* (New York: HarperCollins, 1992), 165.

JUDY CANNATO (1949-2011) was an author, retreat facili-
tator, and spiritual director best known for her work con-
necting the New Cosmology with Christian spirituality. She
was an associate member of the Congregation of St. Joseph
and worked at River's Edge wellness center in Cleveland.
Cannato traveled extensively throughout the United States
giving lectures, workshops, and retreats, and her work was
awarded by the Catholic Press Association. She died after a
battle with cancer on May 7, 2011, and is survived by her
husband and two grown sons.

Founded in 1865, Ave Maria Press,
a ministry of the Congregation of
Holy Cross, is a Catholic publishing
company that serves the spiritual and
formative needs of the Church and its
schools, institutions, and ministers;
Christian individuals and families; and
others seeking spiritual nourishment.

For a complete listing of titles from

Ave Maria Press

Sorin Books

Forest of Peace

Christian Classics

visit www.avemariapress.com

ave maria press® / Notre Dame, IN 46556
A Ministry of the United States Province of Holy Cross